ABRAHAM

Mark E. Petersen

ABRAHAM
Friend of God

Deseret Book Company
Salt Lake City, Utah
1979

Library of Congress Cataloging in Publication Data

Petersen, Mark E
  Abraham, friend of God.

  Includes index.
  1. Abraham, the patriarch. 2. Patriarchs (Bible)
—Biography. 3. Bible. O.T.—Biography.
4. Mormons and Mormonism—Doctrinal and controver-
sial works. I. Title.
BS580.A3P45   222'.11'0924 [B]   79-17445
ISBN 0-87747-780-9

CONTENTS

Chapter 1

BROTHER AGAINST BROTHER

Feuds between brothers are the most bitter of all, and when they extend over generations of time, the scars run deep, seeming never to heal.

Are Jews and Arabs really brothers? Is enmity within that relationship at the seat of their present troubles? Can family strife never end?

Today's conflict in Palestine runs back to a celebration held nearly four thousand years ago in the tents of Abraham, the Friend of God. His favorite son, Isaac, was being weaned; and in accordance with the prevailing custom, the fatted calf was killed and the family held a feast.

Little Isaac and his mother were the center of attention, of course. The boy was a child of divine promise. Nearly half a century before his birth, Abraham and his wife Sarah were told that they would have a son. But Sarah was barren, and through many years they seemed to wait in vain.

When at last Isaac was born, it was indeed a stroke of divine beneficence, for Sarah was now ninety years old and Abraham was a hundred. God had ended her long sterility by a miracle that ignored her time of life. She now had her boy. Her reproach at being childless, a thing dreaded by women of that time and place, was at last removed. With Abraham, she adored her young son.

But all was not well in the family. There was jealousy and anger. To all present at this feast, it was made known that the new babe was Abraham's heir, preferred above the patriarch's only other son, Ishmael, who by now was fourteen years old.

Hagar, the bondwoman, was Ishmael's mother and the second wife of Abraham. She is often referred to as a concubine because of her status as a slave or servant in the house. As preference in favor of Isaac was announced to all at the feast, she was filled with resentment. Already she hated Sarah, but this feeling was now greatly magnified.

Her attitude was reflected in the behavior of Ishmael, who mocked Isaac. Sarah saw what he did and was deeply troubled. Enraged by Ishmael's insult, ''she said unto Abraham, Cast out this bondwoman and her son: for the son of this bondwoman shall not be heir with my son, even with Isaac. And the thing was very grievous in Abraham's sight.'' (Genesis 21:10-11.)

Thus began the conflict that still rages today. Will the Arabs and the Jews never make peace? Is there nothing that can settle their dispute and leave both parties satisfied?

Palestine—the holy land of promise—is the bone of their present contention. Both peoples lay claim to it since both regard Abraham as their eminent progenitor.

The Jews insist that the land is theirs through divine covenant, given by God to their great forefather. But the Arabs do the same, and insist that they are as much blood descendants of Abraham as the Jews. In addition, they claim their right to the land by actual possession. They took it over when the Jews left.

Israel, scattered and hated, allowed centuries to pass by without making so much as an isolated claim to their homeland. So the Arabs moved in, feeling fully justified. Hadn't the Lord made great promises to Ishmael and told him that he as well as Isaac would become a great people, even with royalty arising in his lineage?

The Almighty certainly said that both Isaac and Ishmael would sire nations, princes, and kings. Many nations were to come from Abraham, not Israel alone. Would God discriminate against any one of them, and if so, why?

The Arabs remind the Jews, and none too gently, that Ishmael was the firstborn of Abraham's children, with Isaac second. They ask in all confidence: Do not firstborn sons always enjoy prior rights over others in the family? Is not the firstborn the legal heir?

The Jews rely on scripture to sustain their position. But so do the Arabs— on their own scriptures, which declare Ishmael to be the Lord's prophet and Abraham the founder of the Islamic religion. So again there is a standoff.

Ever since that feast day four thousand years ago, Ishmael

has been the enemy of Isaac, and he still is. The bitterness handed down through the centuries may yet engulf the entire world in war. Will it be Armageddon, involving all nations? It is no wonder that western powers bend every effort to make peace in the Holy Land and avoid further open conflict.

Both sides are fully armed. Both are buying more weapons. And the great nations, including our own, continue to sell every modern instrument of war to the belligerents on both sides. Where will it end?

Chapter 2

THE RISING TIDES

The Arab and Jewish conflict, steadily becoming more complex, is of tremendous concern to the nations of the world.

Both sides have armed themselves heavily, with billions of dollars of aid from the United States and from Russia. Is there any place on earth where there is a greater concentration of fighting gear than in the Middle East?

It seems incredible that so much has been given to so few. Some of the smallest nations in the world are now among the most heavily armed, and they possess the most modern weapons of warfare. Many billions of dollars worth! Both sides are determined to give as little, but to take as much, as possible. Concessions seem to drift further and further from serious consideration.

A remarkable thing has taken place among the Arabs. Their oil money has made a new world for them. The Arab nations have been developing rapidly in industry and agriculture, building schools, educating more of their people, giving more liberty to women, and arming more of their men.

Strangely enough, the modernization movement is running head-on into Islamic religious beliefs that hold to the old traditions, ways, and customs of centuries ago. *U.S. News and World Report* said of this cultural conflict:

"Even in nations where old ways still reign, devout Moslems are trying to counter social change caused by the oil boom and industrialization.

"One instance: In the United Arab Emirates, rising crime and immorality prompted the drafting of a law prohibiting alcohol and decreeing 40 lashes for any Moslem convicted of consuming it. A gambling casino was also closed down. So were bookshops accused of displaying 'material offensive to Moslems.'

"Modernization in the Middle East gets backing from liberal politicians, businessmen and intellectuals who feel that Islam's rigid theology is too committed to the past, not to the rapidly changing present. One Egyptian scholar calls it 'an economic, social and political code for another period.'

"Whatever its problems, Islam is a global faith embracing more than 900 million human beings—including perhaps 3 million, mostly blacks, in the United States.

"Five times daily, the Moslem faithful all over the world kneel to pray, facing Mecca, where the Prophet Mohammed first divulged the new faith. Each year, millions come to Mecca to reaffirm it: 'There is no god but God, and Mohammed is His Prophet.' That creed, as austere and unyielding as the desert that gave it birth, is woven into the fabric of nations where Moslems are in a commanding majority.

"The Sharia, or Koranic law, is still enforced by five governments: Saudi Arabia, Yemen-Sana, Qatar, Libya and the United Arab Emirates state of Abu Dhabi.

"In some of those places, the punishment for theft can be the loss of a hand. Murder, rape and adultery are usually punished by public execution, generally by the sword, but sometimes by stoning or firing squad. Gambling and consumption of alcoholic beverages are forbidden by Koranic law and sometimes punished by flogging.

"Now, however, shock waves—political and social as well as religious—are rolling out from education, travel and an economic revolution.

"Foreigners are introducing pleasures denied to true believers: public displays of affection between the sexes and portrayal of the human image in films and publications."

The most influential Arab state is Saudi Arabia, large in territory and most wealthy of all. That small nation controls a fourth of the world's total supply of oil and is exploring for more. Geologists are confident that more will be found there. *Time* magazine, in an issue largely devoted to the Arabs, said this about the Saudis:

"Its cities are dominated by the roar of bulldozers and the rattle of jackhammers. The hard hat of the construction worker rivals the checkered *ghutra* as the national headdress.

"In the bustling commercial and financial port city of Jidda, on the Red Sea, bulldozers tear into the graceful old houses of the

Ottoman era with their latticework balconies and harem windows. In the capital city of Riyadh, rows of mud houses topped with crenelated roofs are smashed to dust to make way for superhighways or high-rise buildings of chrome, glass and soaring reinforced concrete.

"Passenger jets land and depart from some of the Middle East's busiest airports, shattering the silence of the desert. . . ."

Saudi Arabia has nearly eight million population. Its international monetary reserves amount to more than $40 billion, equal to those of West Germany, and twice those of Great Britain and the United States. Its foreign assets amount to more than $70 billion and are going up at the rate of a billion per month.

The country is building large electric generating plants and providing raw materials for the construction of more homes, better roads, and a number of the elements of a welfare state. The government plans to provide free medical care and now subsidizes food prices to assure a better diet even for the poorest persons. Most of the country's food products are imported. With pupil enrollment increasing, there is a great need for school lunches. Hence the government flies in two hundred thousand meals a day from Paris.

The Saudis are spending more than $6 billion to improve their seaports. They have brought in about a million migrant workers to help with their projects. When contractors come in to build apartment buildings, roads, or electric plants, they must bring in their own crews of workmen, because of the severe labor shortage in that land.

Education has really blossomed in Saudi Arabia. Some 30,000 young Saudis now attend universities, with 20,000 of them studying abroad.

The women of the country are being liberated too, on a large scale. They may now go to school, and many, having been educated, already have entered a variety of businesses. Some also go into medicine. It is estimated that 250,000 Saudi girls are presently in public school, and 11,000 are attending universities, half of whom are studying abroad. Women may not drive cars, however, nor may they travel alone. Polygamy is still a way of life there.

Because the Saudis are so few in number and have the largest area of Arabia to defend, they feel the need of modern fighting gear, and for this reason they are seeking to build a strong air force.

The Arabs are only doing what the Jews have done for a generation or more. Just as the prophets have said, the Holy Land is blossoming as the rose, at least that section controlled by the Jews.

There are many poverty-ridden Arabs inside of Israel. Their lot certainly does not approach that of the Jews. But they are given their freedom, even to vote, and most of them are far better off than their countrymen in the Palestinian-controlled areas.

The Jews have worked miracles in their part of the Holy Land. They possess every modern device. They have the best in schools and some of the best in manufacture. Certainly they excel in agriculture, making crops and trees grow where it seemed impossible before.

One of the remarkable things is the manner in which they have replanted the mountains with cedars. The little seedlings are kept in hothouses at first, then are transplanted with care, sometimes into solid rock with little soil, and there they are made to grow. Millions of trees have been set out successfully in this way. Orchards, groves, and vineyards may be seen in all parts of the land. Even the valley of Armageddon is fertile and productive.

The Israelis own and operate fleets of merchant ships that carry citrus and other foods to various parts of the world, even as far away as Great Britain, which consumes a large part of Israel's farm products.

Women there, of course, work right along with men. There is little difference, even in the tasks allotted to them. They work, they play, they go to war, all on an equal basis.

These are the rising tides that complicate the Middle East picture. These are the elements that make the search for peace increasingly more difficult.

Chapter 3

THE DEATH
OF ENMITY

The conflict between the Arabs and the Jews began with Hagar's marriage to Abraham. From the beginning that marriage was a problem. The union of an Egyptian slave woman and a free Semite man seemed to be incongruous from the start.

Actually, it was an outgrowth of Sarah's disbelief in God's promise that she herself would have a son. She had laughed at the Lord when the promise was given to Abraham, as she hid herself in the family tent. She was old and past the childbearing age and she knew it. And she knew that God knew it.

Abraham's willingness to accept Hagar on the conditions mentioned by Sarah shows his own impatience in waiting for posterity through his first wife as the Lord had promised. As a matter of fact, he had to wait for about fifty years for the promise to be fulfilled. Could he and Sarah be blamed for being impatient?

The hatred that developed in Hagar's heart is understandable since she, as a slave, was called upon to produce children to the name of sterile Sarah.

When Isaac was finally born, Sarah found it unthinkable to consider the son of a bondwoman as an heir of Abraham, a joint heir with her own son. She demanded that Ishmael be barred from any inheritance. Consequently, she banished both him and his mother.

The problem of priority has descended from that day to the present. Were Isaac's progeny to be some kind of super-race? Were Ishmael's descendants to be only second class?

Hagar and Ishmael were faced with this frustration even after the Lord promised Ishmael that he would be the head of a great nation, and that kings and princes would be born of him. They were depressed by the thought that God's covenant was with Isaac and that they were left out of it.

In later years the source of their respective religions also became a bone of contention. The Jews claim that the Islamic religion had its origin in Judaism, which, they charge, the Arabs have corrupted. This the Arabs deny, saying that their religion came by revelation to Mohammed. When the Jews refused to accept Mohammed as a prophet, the Arabs were furious.

Jewish authorities look down upon Mohammed as an interloper. They say that he could not so much as read and write when he began his work. They call him an illiterate camel driver and add that he was laughed out of Mecca when he first claimed to be a prophet. He fled to Medina.

They recount that since many Jews lived in Medina, Mohammed went to them and won their friendship at first by hiding his claims to prophecy. He listened to their Talmud tales and readings from the Torah. He witnessed many of their ceremonies and professed much interest.

They say further that Mohammed hoped to rally the Jews about him, persecuted as they were, when he announced his claim to prophecy. In this he was sadly disappointed. The Jews were a close-knit group, and quickly discerned that Mohammed sought to change their doctrines by placing upon them his own private interpretations. They say he did this to support his claim to a divine call as the founder of Islam. The name Islam, it is said, means "submission to the will of God."

When Mohammed announced that he himself was a prophet, newly raised up by Allah, the Almighty, even his friends among the Jews turned against him. They branded his interpretation of the Torah as "ignorant fraudulent twaddle." Bitterly smarting under this Jewish rejection, "the Prophet of Allah turned furiously against them with the passionate vehemence of a rejected suitor," as Nathan Ausubel explains in the *Book of Jewish Knowledge*. (New York: Crown Publishers, Inc., 1964, p. 224.)

Ausubel then adds: "In the end, Mohammed declared a holy war—a jihad—against the Jews. He avenged himself upon them with fire and sword for the ridicule they had heaped upon him. . . . thousands of Jews [were forced] to dig their own graves in long trenches, where they were decapitated and mutilated." (Ibid.)

He continues: "The Koran makes constant use of Biblical

materials, incidents, legends, and personalities. The stories of
the Pentateuch and the legends about the Prophets, as retold in
the Midrash, furnished Mohammed with the necessary
springboards for the projection of his own religious views and
moral values. He dwells on the story of Creation, Adam and Eve
in the Garden of Eden and their Fall, Cain and the murder of
Abel, the Flood, Noah and the Ark, Abraham and the idols, the
destruction of Sodom, Ishmael and the Angel, and Joseph and his
brothers, etc.'' (Ibid., p. 225.)

In the *Book of Jewish Knowledge* we also read: ''Mohammed
also believed in the imminence of the Day of Judgment (in Hebrew: *Yom ha-Din*; he called it [in Arabic] *Yaum al-Din*). He believed in Paradise and in its fleshly rewards, in Gehinnom
(Gehenna) and in its fiery pits. Like the Providence of God over
Israel, the Providence of Allah was ever spread out protectingly
over the Mohammedan.'' (Ibid., pp. 224-25.)

The Jews accuse the Arabs of reworking many parts of Old
Testament history and leaving them in a jumble. They claim that
the Koran ''hopelessly confuses Moses with Jacob,'' and say the
Arabs believe that Pharaoh commanded the Hebrews to make
bricks to build a tower ''so as to become acquainted with the God
of Moses.''

It is notable that despite the antagonism that has existed between Arabs and Jews, the Arabic language later became vitally
important to the Jews.

Following the return to Jerusalem at the close of the Babylo-
nian captivity, the Jews found that they would have to learn the
Aramaic language, which was literally forced upon them. It was
the common language of the Middle East by now, and had become the chief tongue also of Palestine, which was occupied by
many non-Jews during and after the captivity.

However, author Nathan Ausubel explains that following the
final dispersion in A.D. 70, Arabic—and not Aramaic—became
the spoken language of many of the Jews of the area. Arabic became the literary language in which many Jewish scholars,
philosophers, poets, and scientists composed their works. Hebrew remained the sacred language, however.

Subsequently there developed what has been called the
Arabic-Jewish Golden Age in North Africa, Babylonia, and

Southern Spain. This occurred during the ninth to fourteenth centuries as Arabic culture supplanted the Greek in that area and the Jews accepted it. Both Jews and Arabs of that region retained their separate religious ideas, but cooperated in nearly every other cultural activity. During this period, according to Ausubel, the ranks of Jewish scholars, scientists, and poets swelled ''to the proportion of a small army.'' (Ibid., pp. 10-11.)

Due to the dispersion, of course, the Jews had scattered to nearly all parts of the world, with but few still remaining in the Palestine area.

Following World War I, with the signing of the Balfour treaty and with the cooperation of Britain and the United States, the Jews began returning to their homeland. This naturally enraged the Arabs, for large numbers of them were thereby dispossessed of their lands, giving rise to the present Palestinian problem. As displaced persons, they had to move out of what for centuries had been their own homeland.

Any happy relationships that existed during the Middle Ages were quickly turned to animosity, which seems to grow now, day by day, with each new confrontation.

Are the Jews entitled to Palestine? Are the Arabs?

Displaced Jews and displaced Palestinians both demand a homeland in the same little bit of ground. Their hatred seems to preclude their living together. They appear to have little mutual tolerance.

Can Isaac and Ishmael never be brothers indeed?

Chapter 4

WHO ARE "OF ABRAHAM"?

The Lord said to Abraham: "I will make thee exceeding fruitful, and I will make nations of thee, and kings shall come out of thee." (Genesis 17:6.)

When he spoke to Abraham concerning Sarah, he said: "I will bless her, and she shall be a mother of nations; kings of people shall be of her." (Genesis 17:16.)

And to Hagar the divine promise came: "I will make him [Ishmael] a great nation." (Genesis 21:18.)

The Lord previously had said to Abraham: "Also of the son of the bondwoman will I make a nation, because he is thy seed." (Genesis 21:13.)

Again the Lord said to Abraham: "As for Ishmael, I have heard thee: Behold, I have blessed him, and will make him fruitful, and will multiply him exceedingly; twelve princes shall he beget, and I will make him a great nation." However, the Lord added, "But my covenant will I establish with Isaac, which Sarah shall bear unto thee." (Genesis 17:20-21.) At this point the Lord narrowed the chosen lineage.

Nations, kings, princes, and multitudes were to come from Abraham through both Isaac and Ishmael—*but* the Lord's covenant would be with Isaac.

This was confirmed when the Lord spoke further to Abraham as he grieved over the dispute between Sarah and Hagar, and the future of his son Ishmael. The Lord said: "Let it not be grievous in thy sight because of the lad [Ishmael], and because of thy bondwoman; in all that Sarah hath said unto thee, hearken unto her voice; for in Isaac shall thy seed be called." (Genesis 21:12.)

There was no misunderstanding that language. Ishmael would be greatly blessed, but the covenant was to be with Isaac. The Lord was obviously selecting a particular parentage for his chosen people, and Ishmael's descendants were not included.

This principle was repeated in the selection of Jacob over Esau. Again the covenant was only with Jacob. Esau too was to become a great people, but as the Lord had said to Abraham, "In Isaac thy seed shall be called," even so now it was in Jacob that "thy seed shall be called." (Genesis 27.) Only in Isaac! Only in Jacob!

There was a definite narrowing of the "the seed." The lineage of Abraham, though accounting for many nations, had but one select line in which the special blessings were promised.

Why were some thus favored over others? Was not the Lord always just? The scriptures make it clear that he is no respecter of persons. What is the explanation?

President Joseph Fielding Smith, in his book *The Way to Perfection*, says: "Our place among the tribes and nations evidently was assigned to us by the Lord. That there was an assignment of this kind before earth-life began, is a declaration in the scriptures. Certain spirits were chosen to come through the lineage of Abraham, and this choice was made in the beginning. Other selections were also made and the nations determined upon by the councils in the heavens."

Then President Smith quotes Paul's speech on Mars' Hill wherein the ancient apostle said that the Almighty "hath made of one blood all nations of men for to dwell on all the face of the earth, and hath determined the times before appointed, and the bounds of their habitation." (Acts 17:26.)

President Smith continues: "If the Lord appointed unto the nations the bounds of their habitations, then there must have been a selection of spirits to form these nations. In greater clearness Moses has declared the same thing."

Then he quotes the following words of Moses:

"Remember the days of old, consider the years of many generations: ask thy father, and he will shew thee; thy elders, and they will tell thee.

"When the most High divided to the nations their inheritance, when he separated the sons of Adam, he set the bounds of the people according to the number of the children of Israel.

"For the Lord's portion is his people; Jacob is the lot of his inheritance." (Deuteronomy 32:7-9.)

With further explanation President Smith says: "If bounds

were set according to the number of the children of Israel, and they were the Lord's portion (i.e., those with whom he made covenant), when the Lord divided the sons of Adam, it must have been done before this earth-life began. For in these days of old when this division was made, the nation of Israel had not been brought into existence on earth.''

President Smith then goes on to explain that our preexistent behavior most likely determined which spirits would be born through Isaac and Jacob. He says: "However, we must not be unmindful of the fact, that these world conditions have also been brought about in large degree by rebellion and disregard of the laws of God in this life. Retrogression has come upon mankind because they have rejected the counsels and commandments of the Almighty. Advancement has come largely because men have been willing to walk, in part at least, in the light of divine inspiration. Moreover, notwithstanding the fact that the Lord chose a certain nation as his "portion" and that Jacob became the "lot of his inheritance," the Almighty also was kind to other nations and leavened them by scattering the blood of Israel among them. In this and other ways the nations became blessed as the seed of Abraham.'' (*The Way to Perfection*, Genealogical Society of Utah, 1949, pp. 46-48.)

President Harold B. Lee spoke in similar vein:

". . . many were chosen, as was Abraham, before they were born, as the Lord told Moses and also Jeremiah. This was made still more meaningful by the latter-day prophet, Joseph Smith, who declared that 'every person who is called to do an important work in the kingdom of God, was called to that work and foreordained to that work before the world was.' Then he added, 'I believe that I was foreordained to the work that I am called to do.' (See *History of the Church* 6:364.)

"But now there is a warning: Despite that calling which is spoken of in the scriptures as 'foreordination,' we have another inspired declaration: 'Behold, there are many called, but few are chosen.' (D&C 121:34.)

"This suggests that even though we have our free agency here, there are many who were foreordained before the world was, to a greater state than they have prepared themselves for here. Even though they might have been among the noble and great, from among whom the Father declared he would make his chosen leaders, they may fail of that calling here in mortality. Then the Lord poses this question: 'And why are they not chosen?' (D&C 121:34.)

"Two answers were given: First, 'Because their hearts are set so much upon the things of this world. . . .' And second, they '. . . aspire to the honors of men.' (D&C 121:35.)

"Now then, to summarize, may I ask each of you again the question, 'Who are you?' You are all the sons and daughters of God. Your spirits were created and lived as organized intelligences before the world was. You have been blessed to have a physical body because of your obedience to certain commandments in that premortal state. You are now born into a family to which you have come, into the nations through which you have come, as a reward for the kind of lives you lived before you came here and at a time in the world's history, as the Apostle Paul taught the men of Athens and as the Lord revealed to Moses, determined by the faithfulness of each of those who lived before this world was created."

President Lee quotes Deuteronomy 32:8, as referred to by Paul on Mars' Hill and then says: "Now, mind you, this was said to the children of Israel before they had arrived in the Promised Land, which was to be the land of their inheritance.

"Then note this next verse: 'For the Lord's portion is his people; Jacob is the lot of his inheritance.' (Deuteronomy 32:9.)

"It would seem very clear, then, that those born to the lineage of Jacob, who was later to be called Israel, and his posterity, who were known as the children of Israel, were born into the most illustrious lineage of any of those who came upon the earth as mortal beings.

"All these rewards were seemingly promised, or foreordained, before the world was. Surely these matters must have been determined by the kind of lives we had lived in that premortal spirit world. Some may question these assumptions, but at the same time they will accept without any question the belief that each one of us will be judged when we leave this earth according to his or her deeds during our lives here in mortality. Isn't it just as reasonable to believe that what we have received here in this earth life was given to each of us according to the merits of our conduct before we came here?'' (*Stand Ye in Holy Places*, Deseret Book, 1975, pp. 9-11.)

President Joseph Fielding Smith continued his explanation as follows:

"In the parable of the talents the Lord makes use of this very significant expression: 'For the kingdom of heaven is as a man traveling into a far country, who called his own servants, and delivered unto them his goods. And unto one he gave five talents, to another two and to another one; to every man according to his several ability.' Without doubt, these characteristics were born with us. In other words, we developed certain traits of character in the world of spirits before this earth-life began. In that life some were more diligent in the performance of duty. Some were more obedient and faithful in keeping the commandments. Some were more intellectual, and others manifested stronger traits of leadership than others. Some showed greater faith and willingness to serve the Lord, and from among these the leaders were chosen.

"Because of this condition the Lord said to Abraham:

" 'These I will make my rulers; for he stood among those that were spirits, and he saw that they were good; and he said unto me: Abraham, thou art one of them; thou wast chosen before thou wast born.' (Abraham 3:23.)

"There must be leaders, presiding officers, and those who are worthy and able to take command. During the ages in which we dwelt in the pre-mortal state we not only developed our various characteristics and showed our worthiness and ability, or the lack of it, but we were also where such progress could be observed. It is reasonable to believe that there was a Church organization there. The heavenly beings were living in a perfectly arranged society. Every person knew his place. Priesthood, without any question, had been conferred and the leaders were chosen to officiate. Ordinances pertaining to that pre-existence were required and the love of God prevailed. Under such conditions it was natural for our Father to discern and choose those who were most worthy and evaluate the talents of each individual. He knew not only what each of us *could* do, but also what each of us *would* do when put to the test and when responsibility was given us. Then, when the time came for our habitation on mortal earth, all things were prepared and the servants of the Lord chosen and ordained to their respective missions.

"Paul said to the Ephesian Saints:

" ' Blessed be the God and Father of our Lord Jesus Christ, who hath blessed us with all spiritual blessings in heavenly places in Christ:

" 'According as he hath chosen us in him before the foundation of the world, that we should be holy and without blame before him in love.' (Ephesians 1:3-4.)

"It was because the Father understood these characteristics, and the abilities of the spirits before him, that he was able to choose his rulers as 'he stood in the midst of them' before the earth was born." (*The Way to Perfection*, pp. 50-51.)

President Smith refers to the "wonderful compliment" the Lord paid to Abraham in these words:

"For I know him, that he will command his children and his household after him, and they shall keep the way of the Lord, to do justice and judgment; that the Lord may bring upon Abraham that which he hath spoken of him. (Genesis 18:19.)

"This could be said of Abraham because he was known as 'faithful' as he stood in the midst of the intelligences before the world was, for it was there that he was chosen as one of the great ones to be a ruler on the earth." (Ibid., p. 53.)

Chapter 5

ISLAM AND ABRAHAM

Descent from Abraham is quite as sacred to the Arabs as it is to the Jews. This is made abundantly clear in the Koran and the other teachings of Mohammed.

Mohammed, or Muhammed as the Koran spells the name, said:

"O People of the Scripture! Why will ye argue about Abraham, when the Torah and the Gospel were not revealed till after him? Have ye then no sense?

"Lo! ye are those who argue about that whereof ye have some knowledge: Why then argue ye concerning that whereof ye have no knowledge? Allah knoweth. Ye know not.

"Abraham was not a Jew, nor yet a Christian; but he was an upright man who had surrendered to Allah, and he was not of the idolaters.

"Lo! those of mankind who have the best claim to Abraham are those who followed him, and this Prophet [Mohammed] and those who believe with him; and Allah is the Protecting Friend of the believers." (Koran, Surah III:65-68.)

Mohammed claims that Abraham was the founder of Islam and that he actually built the sacred Islamic sanctuary at Mecca. So we quote:

"And remember when his Lord tried Abraham with His commands, and he fulfilled them, He said: Lo! I have appointed thee a leader for mankind. Abraham said, And of my offspring will there be leaders? He said, My covenant includeth not wrongdoers.

"And when We made the House at Mecca a resort for mankind and a sanctuary, saying: Take as your place of worship where Abraham stood to pray. And We imposed a duty upon Abraham and Ishmael, saying: Purify My house for those who go around and those who meditate therein and those who bow down and prostrate themselves in worship.

"And when Abraham prayed: My Lord! Make this [Mecca] a region of security and bestow upon its people fruits, such as them as believe in Allah and the Last Day, He answered: As for him who disbelieveth, I shall leave him in contentment for a while, then I shall compel him to the doom of fire—a hapless journey's end!

"And when Abraham and Ishmael were raising the foundations of the House, Abraham prayed: Our Lord, Accept from us this duty. Lo, Thou, only Thou, art the Hearer, the Knower." (Surah II:124-127.)

At another time the Koran says: "We shall worship thy God, the God of thy fathers Abraham and Ishmael and Isaac, One God, and unto him we have surrendered." (Surah II:133.)

We also read this:

"Say O Muslims: We believe in Allah and that which is revealed unto us and that which was revealed unto Abraham, and Ishmael, and Isaac, and Jacob, and the tribes, and that which Moses and Jesus received, and that which the Prophets received from their Lord. *We make no distinction between any of them* and unto Him have we surrendered." (Surah II:136. Italics added.)

As further evidence that Arabs believe that their religion traces back to Abraham, we read: "Who is better in religion than he who surrendereth his purposes to Allah while doing good to men and followeth the tradition of Abraham, the upright? Allah Himself chose Abraham for friend." (Surah IV:125.)

In Surah IV:163 we read that Allah inspired Abraham, Ishmael, Isaac, and Jacob. At various times the text indicates that there is no distinction drawn between them.

Surah V:76-84 declares that Allah showed Abraham the stars of the heavens in the nighttime and discussed with him the greater ones.

Another interesting passage written by Mohammed, as though quoting Abraham, is this: "Praise be to Allah, who hath given me, in my old age, Ishmael and Isaac! Lo! my Lord is indeed the Hearer of Prayer." (Surah XIV:39.)

Not only do they regard themselves as descendants of Ishmael and place him equal with Isaac, but the Arabs also believe Ishmael was one of Allah's prophets:

"And make mention in the Scripture of Ishmael. Lo! he was the keeper of his promise, and he was a messenger of Allah, a

Prophet. He enjoined upon his people worship and almsgiving, and was acceptable in the sight of his Lord.'' (Surah XIX:54-55.)

In *Smith's Bible Dictionary* (2:978) we are told that ''in Mohammedan tradition, Hagar is represented as the wife [not the concubine] of Abraham.'' This is as might be expected, when we remember that Ishmael is the head of the Arab nation and the reputed ancestor of Mohammed. They refuse to put Hagar in a secondary position.

Among the legends of the Muslims, God is said to have commanded Abraham to go to Mecca with Ishmael to build a temple there. It is said also that the angel Gabriel was sent to give Abraham and Ishmael instructions regarding the sanctuary and the conduct of pilgrimages to it.

The *Times and Seasons*, an early Latter-day Saint publication edited by Parley P. Pratt and his brother Orson, carried an article on the Arabs and their relationship to Ishmael under date of August 15, 1845, of which the following is an excerpt:

''The history of the Arabs, so opposite in many respects to that of the Jews, but as singular as theirs, was concisely and clearly foretold.—It was prophesied concerning Ishmael:—'He will be a wild man; his hand will be against every man, and every man's hand against him; and he shall dwell in the presence of all his brethren. I will make him fruitful, and will multiply him exceedingly; and I will make him a great nation.' (Genesis 16:12; 17:20.)

''The fate of Ishmael is here identified with that of his descendants; and the same character is common to them both. The historical evidence of the fact, the universal tradition, and constant boast of the Arabs themselves, their language, and preservation for many ages of an original rite, derived from him as their primogenitor, confirm the truth of their descent from Ishmael. The fulfillment of the prediction is obvious. . . .

''The independence of the Arabs was proverbial in ancient as well as in modern times; and the present existence, as a free and independent nation, of a people who derive their descent from so high antiquity, demonstrates that they have never been wholly subdued, as all the nations around them have unquestionably been; and that they have ever dwelt in the presence of their brethren.

"They not only subsist unconquered to this day, but the prophesied and primitive wildness of their race, and their hostility to all, remains unsubdued and unaltered. 'They are a wild people; their hand is against every man; and every man's hand is against them.'

"In the words of Gibbon, which strikingly assimilate with those of the prophecy, they are *'armed* against mankind.'...

"Their alliance is never courted, and can never be obtained; and all that the Turks, or Persians, or any of their neighbors, can stipulate for from them, is a partial and purchased forbearance.

"Even the British, who have established a residence in almost every country, have entered the territories of the descendants of Ishmael to accomplish only the premeditated destruction of a fort and to retire. It cannot be alleged with truth, that their peculiar character and manner, and its interrupted permanency, are the necessary results of the nature of their country....

"The greatest part of the temperate zone was included within the limits of the Arabian conquests; and their empire extended from the confines of India to the shores of the Atlantic, and embrace a wider range of territory than ever was passed by the Romans, those boasted masters of the world.—

"The period of their conquest and dominion was sufficient, under such circumstances, to have changed the manners of any people: but, whether in the land of Shinah, or in the valleys of Spain, on the banks of the Tigris, or the Tagus, in Arabia the blessed, or Arabia, the barren, the posterity of Ishmael have ever maintained their prophetic character....

"The natural reflection of a recent traveler, on examining the peculiarities of an Arab tribe, of which he was an eye-witness, may suffice, without any art of controversy, for the illustration of this prophecy: 'On the smallest computation, such must have been the manners of those people for more than three thousand years: thus in all things verifying the prediction given of Ishmael at his birth....

"And that an acute and active people, surrounded for ages by polished and luxurious nations, should from their earliest to their latest times, be still found a wild people, dwelling in the presence of all their brethren, (as we may call those nations,) unsubdued and unchangeable, is indeed a standing miracle; one of those mysterious facts which establish the truth of prophecy.''

According to Mohammed, Abraham was one of the early advocates of monotheism and fully recognized Allah as the creator.

The Arabs have perpetuated certain myths about Abraham, admitting, however, that the stories are mere legends. One legend concerned Nimrod, the ''god-king'' of Babylonia, who had been warned through astrology that a child would be born in Ur to dethrone him. That infant was Abraham. The king thereupon decreed that all infants of the realm were to be killed. However, Abraham was hidden in a cave and was nursed there by the angel Gabriel. He was said to have been such a precocious child that within a few days of his birth he was able to both walk and talk.

Another Arabian story relates that Abraham in his youth studied under Shem, son of Noah; that together they created a person out of earth and water; and that the figure was made to live and speak.

Islam reveres one tradition especially, for it shows Abraham as a sincere worshipper of the true God despite all opposition, and states that he willingly submitted to persecution rather than to give up his faith.

Chapter 6

JEHOVAH AND ALLAH

Jehovah is the God of the Jews. Allah is worshipped by the Arabs. Are they one and the same? What did this Almighty Being teach, war or peace?

Were his instructions of one kind to the Jews and of another to the Arabs? Was there not some common ground in the divine teachings on which the two brother nations could find peace and do so even now? Or do they believe their respective religions sufficiently to apply the sacred precepts?

Allah taught the brotherhood of man. "Allah is forgiving; Allah is merciful," he said. He taught his believers to be kind and considerate.

Actually the Koran reads: "Righteous is he who believeth in Allah and the Last Day and the angels and the scripture and the Prophets; and giveth his wealth for love of Him to kinsfolk and to orphans and the needy and the wayfarer and to those who ask, and to set slaves free; and observeth proper worship and payeth the poor due." (Surah II:177.)

He taught mankind to love one another "with a love like that which is due to Allah only." (Surah II:165.)

In directing all worshippers to face toward Mecca as they pray, he taught them the value of justice. He said: "Whencesoever thou comest forth turn thy face toward the Inviolable Place of Worship and wheresoever ye may be, O Muslims, turn your faces toward it when ye pray so that men may have no argument against you save such of them as do injustice—Fear not them, but fear me." (Surah II:150.)

So the deity of the Arabs teaches brotherly love, justice, charity, generosity, and kindness.

What of Jehovah of the Jews?

He it was who taught the Golden Rule and love of neighbor as of self. He it was who taught charity, mercy, and forgiveness.

His principles were firm and direct:

"Ye shall not steal, neither deal falsely, neither lie one to another.

"And ye shall not swear by my name falsely, neither shalt thou profane the name of thy God: I am the Lord.

"Thou shalt not defraud thy neighbor, neither rob him: the wages of him that is hired shall not abide with thee all night until the morning.

"Thou shalt not curse the deaf, nor put a stumblingblock before the blind, but shalt fear thy God: I am the Lord.

"Ye shall do no unrighteousness in judgment: thou shalt not respect the person of the poor, nor honour the person of the mighty: but in righteousness shalt thou judge thy neighbour.

"Thou shalt not go up and down as a talebearer among thy people: neither shalt thou stand against the blood of thy neighbour: I am the Lord.

"Thou shalt not hate thy brother in thine heart: thou shalt in any wise rebuke thy neighbour, and not suffer sin upon him.

"Thou shalt not avenge, nor bear any grudge against the children of thy people, but thou shalt love thy neighbour as thyself: I am the Lord." (Leviticus 19:11-18.)

Not only that, but the great Jehovah, God of the Old Testament, further declared: "He that killeth any man shall surely be put to death." (Leviticus 24:17.)

Are not these teachings of both Jehovah and Allah the necessary common ground?

And what of Abraham, the progenitor of both races? Did he teach war, or was he a peaceful man, willing to hold out the olive branch on any sound basis?

Abraham was the Friend of God, acknowledged so by both Koran and Bible, by both Arabs and Jews. The Friend of God! Would he be an enemy to the divine law? Was not Abraham a believer in all the virtues that both sets of scriptures set forth? What did he say?

"I sought for the blessings of the fathers . . .; having been myself a follower of righteousness, desiring also . . . to keep the commandments of God, I became a rightful heir, a High Priest, holding the right belonging to the fathers." (Abraham 1:2.)

He taught repentance to his family and neighbors who had

turned "unto the worshiping of the gods of the heathen" although they "utterly refused to hearken to my voice." (Abraham 1:5.) Why do not the Jews and Arabs accept his word? But they will not so far as their interrelationships are concerned.

Even if Abraham were to come back from the dead today, would anyone believe him? Would they put down their arms and make peace on the grounds of their own respective religious teachings?

A sinner once cried out to Father Abraham in heaven seeking mercy. The story goes like this:

"There was a certain rich man, which was clothed in purple and fine linen, and fared sumptuously every day:

"And there was a certain beggar named Lazarus, which was laid at his gate, full of sores,

"And desiring to be fed with the crumbs which fell from the rich man's table: moreover the dogs came and licked his sores.

"And it came to pass, that the beggar died, and was carried by the angels into Abraham's bosom: the rich man also died, and was buried;

"And in hell he lift up his eyes, being in torments, and seeth Abraham afar off, and Lazarus in his bosom.

"And he cried and said, Father Abraham, have mercy on me, and send Lazarus, that he may dip the tip of his finger in water, and cool my tongue; for I am tormented in this flame.

"But Abraham said, Son, remember that thou in thy lifetime receivedst thy good things, and likewise Lazarus evil things: but now he is comforted, and thou art tormented.

"And beside all this, between us and you there is a great gulf fixed: so that they which would pass from hence to you cannot; neither can they pass to us, that would come from thence.

"Then he said, I pray thee therefore, father, that thou wouldest send him to my father's house:

"For I have five brethren; that he may testify unto them, lest they also come into this place of torment.

"Abraham saith unto him, They have Moses and the prophets; let them hear them.

"And he said, Nay, father Abraham: but if one went unto them from the dead, they will repent.

"And he said unto him, If they hear not Moses and the

prophets, neither will they be persuaded, though one rose from the dead.'' (Luke 16:19-31.)

Who is Jehovah? Who is Allah? Both are worshipped by millions. Are they one and the same, but with different names? Both are spoken of by their followers as the One God, the Creator of the worlds. Both are reported to have walked and talked with Abraham. Both made him ''friend.'' The One God means all of that to both sides.

Both are said to have inspired the prophets, giving revelations for the good of man. Only faith in the true God can solve their problem. But where is such faith? Where are people who are willing to accept their religions as a true way of life, and not something to be set aside for political considerations?

Christians cannot be left out of it either, for Christ taught the Golden Rule. He taught us to love our neighbors as ourselves, to be kind, merciful, and forgiving.

And who is Christ? He is the Almighty, the Creator of heaven and earth. He is Jehovah of the Old Testament, and if the Arabs only knew and would accept it, he is their God and their Creator too. There is no salvation in any other!

Jesus the Christ is the God of love. He is the Prince of Peace. But is anyone humble enough to live the divine principles of peace?

In the Middle East today we have had Christians fighting Jews, both of them fighting Arabs, and Arabs shooting Christians and Jews. Religion does not enter the picture. It is allowed no quarter, no area of refuge nor room for sane discussion. Political expediency is all that seems to matter. Selfishness is the controlling factor.

It was very much like that in the beginning with Abraham's first children. Which of the two boys endeavored to love his neighbor or his brother as himself? Which of them held to the Golden Rule? Which of them showed any filial affection?

And we have never been willing to learn the divine lessons since. What does that say for the faith of humanity in their Creator and their God?

Chapter 7

THE
MELTING POT

The Arab-Jewish conflict even reaches the United States because America is a melting pot. People from all nations have come to America for a better life. They have obtained great opportunities for individual advancement, which are fruits of the precious liberty of this land.

In America people from many countries have learned to live together in peace and harmony. Former national lines have disappeared; people have given up their past allegiance and have become Americans, fellow citizens in this land of the free.

This one factor has in it the full possibility of making world peace. In America it is proven that different nationalities can live together in harmony, that they can put away their prejudices and accept a common ground.

This is a lesson that all the world might learn from America if they will. It is a lesson that even today the Jews and the Arabs might study.

Millions of Jews and Arabs live in America. They do so without interracial strife. Their differences are seldom mentioned and never expressed in violence. They have learned to become Americans, to put their Americanism first.

With so many Arabs and Jews residing in America, could they not become a leaven in the lump for helping to bring peace to their homelands? But this has not been done thus far. Quite the opposite. Melting-pot-Americanism has been forgotten to a great extent among those of both sides now in the U.S. Their former native patriotism, with all its strong prejudices and demands, has surfaced once again. But even so, there is no physical violence between them in this land.

It is said that there are more Jews in New York than in any other city in the world. Altogether there are nearly six million in the United States. According to a recent U.S. census report,

3,050,000 were in New York and the Middle Atlantic states; 908,000 in the South; 763,000 in the West; 720,000 in the Midwest; and 405,000 in New England.

But what of the Arabs? Have they come to America in any number?

With all their "oil money" they are not only in the U.S., but they are also investing heavily in American business. There are about two million Arabs in the United States with the largest concentration in Detroit, which is sometimes called the mother city of Arab-Americans. Other concentrations of Arabs are in Los Angeles, Houston, Chicago, and New York, where there are also many Jews.

While the Arabs have not lobbied a great deal in American political circles, the Jews have been very active in this regard. With several Jews in the U.S. Senate, and about three dozen separate lobbying groups, each with an office in Washington, the Jews in America wield considerable clout. The Arabs and their friends are learning from other lobbying groups, however, and are beginning to make their influence felt. They pay huge sums to public relations firms to shape American public opinion in their favor. But they avoid violence. As a result, some Congressmen have begun to advocate the Arab side and are beginning to reexamine their former support of the Israeli cause.

There is no doubt but that the oil interests in the Arab nations have changed much of the thinking in America, as have the arms sales to both Israelis and Arabs.

So in the United States as in the Near East itself, the conflict between the two groups goes bitterly on. But still they do not attack each other physically in this land. They have found some common ground in America for peaceful coexistence.

The big difficulty with peace between Jews and Arabs, whether in America or in Palestine, is that the problem is constantly kept on a selfish political basis. Why don't both sides try to practice their respective religions, and make peace as sincere believers in one God who teaches love and brotherhood? Religious belief is supposed to be controlling in the lives of both. Then let it be!

The Koran commands brotherly love as much as does the Bible. Mohammed taught it as earnestly as the Jewish prophets.

Why do not both sides put their religion to work?

In the spirit of the Golden Rule any conflict can be settled, but when believers in God refuse to apply their own religious teachings in dealing with other peoples, then their faith seems not to run very deep. Is there never a thought of turning the other cheek? Must reprisals and revenge be the controlling factors forever?

Allah is the God of the Arabs. Jehovah is the God of the Jews. Do not the teachings of both provide the common ground they need for a peaceful settlement?

But Arabs and Jews are quite like many Christians in this regard. They don't let their religion interfere with their daily lives. Some of the world's worst wars have been fought between the Christians themselves. In the last two world wars, Christians fought each other to the death. Sometimes fathers were pitted against their own sons, all being Christians, all fighting for their political rights, all praying to the same God for victory.

The wars of the past have not been different in their motives. Will anyone forget when Christian slaughtered Christian as the unfortunate Huguenots of the sixteenth and seventeenth centuries were wiped out in France?

Can any Christian be proud of the Thirty-Year War, or of the repeated conflicts between Christian France and Christian England, for example?

After all is said, when wars are thrust upon the populace, religion seems to be very thin indeed. This is especially true of those who love and make and promote wars that bring untold misery upon millions of helpless victims. No one wins a war. All suffer. Yet mankind never learns its lesson.

There is peace to be obtained if we will be willing to pay for it, but lasting peace is not paid for in money or territory or prestige. Its price is living our religion, loving our neighbors as ourselves, and doing to them as we would be done by.

This principle was ignored by Hagar and Sarah, by Ishmael and Isaac, and by their descendants down through the many generations. Does either side think of it today?

Chapter 8

THE JEWS AND ABRAHAM

To the Jews, Abraham is indeed the father of the faithful, and particularly is he the father of Israel. He was the friend of God and is regarded as the greatest of their ancestors.

The sacrifice of Isaac is considered to be his greatest test and is accepted by the Jews as a fact, not a myth. They hold it up as an ideal example for all to follow in mind and heart, although no one else may ever be called upon to go to the length that Abraham did.

The Talmud and the Torah sustain the tradition of Abraham as the founder of the Jewish race. They perpetuate the promises made repeatedly by the Almighty during the years Abraham was in Mesopotamia and later in Palestine.

The Jews give little credence to the Arab claims to the Holy Land since it was a fact, they say, that Abraham willed only gifts to the children of his concubines and then sent them away. (Genesis 25:5-6.) They say that such children could in no way be heirs to the promise because they were without status. Therefore, they have no legitimate claim to the land. Isaac, they insist, was the only one given a legacy.

It is acknowledged that the Arabs possessed Palestine for centuries after the Jewish dispersion, but the Jews point out that they were compelled to leave and were not allowed to exercise any option. They were scattered by force and had no opportunity to recover their land until after World War I, when the British under General Edmund Allenby took it from the Turks.

To the Jews Abraham achieved the highest level in prophecy, although some add "with the possible exception of Moses." They credit Abraham with having been the first to promote the idea of a special creation of the world by a single God as contrasted with the views of polytheism.

One of the great Jewish philosophers, Maimonides, however, says that Abraham proved the existence of God only by the power of reasoning, and that the patriarch accepted the existence of divinity largely because of the order he observed in the planetary movements and the fixed position of the stars.

The Jews have venerated Abraham both in literature and in music. Many paintings of Israel, as well as those of Islam, show him in the pose of sacrificing Isaac, while others also follow Islam in depicting Abraham being saved from the fiery furnace of King Nimrod. It seems that among certain Jews this legend is accepted equally with the Arabs.

Several musical compositions by Jews are based on the life of Abraham, some appearing as early as the seventeenth century. One of them, Scarlatti's *Agar et Ismaeli Esiliati*, was written in 1683. It tells the story of Hagar and Ishmael, as the title indicates. One of Schubert's first songs, written in 1811, was "Hagar's Klage." In 1806 Etienne Nicolas Mehul wrote an opera on the theme *Agar au Desert*.

Abraham's youth formed the theme for a work by Michael Gnessin, written during a visit to Israel in 1922. Various other Jewish musical compositions have appeared during the past forty years.

The *Encyclopedia Britannica* says this about Abraham:

"In rabbinic tradition Abraham occupies a position of eminence. His faith atones for the sins of Israel, and he was even the rock upon which God built and established the world. In the New Testament, allusions are made to this role of Abraham; *e.g.*, in Matt. viii, 11 and Luke xiii, 28-29, where Abraham is an eschatological figure, represented as the host at the heavenly banquet (cf. Luke xvi, 22). The promises to Abraham are recognized as giving the Jews a special prerogative (Rom. ix, 8; xi, 1 ff.). Yet, being children of Abraham has a spiritual, rather than a national, meaning (Rom. ix, 7 ff.; cf. Gal. iii, 9).

"The true children of Abraham are 'children of the promise' (Rom. ix, 8), and that promise is fulfilled in Christ (Gal. iii, 14). Thus Abraham becomes a precursor of Christ. In Him the promises to Abraham are fulfilled (Gal. iii, 25-29; cf. Heb. vii), and Christians, even the gentile ones, partake in the blessing in Abraham (Gal. iii, 8 ff.; cf. Gen. xii, 3).

"Paul seizes upon Abraham's righteousness by faith (Gen.

xv, 6) in order to expound his central thesis that righteousness is granted through faith rather than through works (Rom. iv, 1 ff.; Gal. iii, 6 ff.). In the epistle to the Hebrews, Abraham is an example of the faith that receives God's promise and responds to it in obedience (Heb. xi, 8 ff.)." (*Encyclopaedia Britannica*, Chicago: Wm. Benton, 1966, 1:45.)

This publication relegates much of the tradition about Abraham to the field of "less than history," or folklore. It goes on to say:

"How much can be stated about Abraham as a historical person? Abraham and the other patriarchs have sometimes been considered to be personifications of clans or even figures of myth. This opinion has been proved erroneous.

"To be sure, the story of Abraham in the Bible is not a biography in the modern sense of the word. The ancients told stories of persons in order to illuminate the meaning of the clan's or the nation's life. Yet, there can be no doubt that Abraham existed. On the other hand, it is not possible to be specific either about when he lived or about the details of his life.

"Excavations at Mari on the Euphrates, at Nuzi and elsewhere have yielded texts which illuminate customs, names and tribal history in the first half of the 2nd millennium B.C.; it has become evident that the narratives about Abraham in the Bible authentically reflect that age (perhaps the 18th-17th centuries B.C.).

"Abraham was a seminomad who belonged perhaps to a social stratum called Habiru (cf. the word 'Hebrew,' possibly from the same root, in Gen. xiv, 13)."

All of this, of course, merely emphasizes the value of the modern revelations possessed by the Latter-day Saints concerning Abraham, which make of him a real person, a great prophet, and actually a "friend of God."

Chapter 9

TRULY, WHO WAS ABRAHAM?

Was Abraham, so surrounded by mythology, really a person? Did he live and breathe and walk and talk with God? Or has he been plucked out of the legendary recesses of antiquity to help mold unity into an afflicted and persecuted people of today?

Is he now being brought into modern prominence merely to help settle a present-day argument over territorial possessions?

When it comes to basic proof of his identity, the Latter-day Saints have the only solid facts in the matter, and what they have has been received by revelation as the sheer word of God.

Revelation—modern revelation in particular—is the key to solving what scholars regard as the "mystery of Abraham." Some archaeological findings are pointed to, but even they are not conclusive. More and more the researchers are admitting that the patriarch existed. But they say there is so little either in history or solid research that no concrete story of his life may be assembled.

But not so with the Latter-day Saints. By revelation through the Prophet Joseph Smith, we know that Abraham lived and ministered here on earth. He was a potent factor in the Lord's plans for Israel, for us as modern children of Abraham, and for the world at large who yet will be blessed through him and his seed.

By revelation we know that indeed Abraham was the friend of God, and that he was divinely chosen to occupy his important position on earth even before he was born into mortality.

Not only was he a friend of God in earth life, but he also was a friend of God in premortal life, for as the scripture says, he was one of the great ones there. "These I will make my rulers," the Almighty had said, adding, "Abraham, thou art one of them; thou wast chosen before thou wast born." (Abraham 3:23.)

Just as Jeremiah was chosen before he was born, so was

Abraham. The scripture referring to Jeremiah is most interesting, showing that not only was he chosen before his birth, but that he was also ordained a prophet in that primeval period: ''Before I formed thee in the belly I knew thee; and before thou camest forth out of the womb I sanctified thee, and I ordained thee a prophet unto the nations.'' (Jeremiah 1:5.)

The Prophet Joseph Smith said this concerning such ordinations: ''Every man who has a calling to minister to the inhabitants of the world was ordained to that very purpose in the Grand Council of heaven before this world was. I suppose that I was ordained to this very office in that Grand Council.''(HC 6:364.)

To Latter-day Saints, then, Abraham was just as real a person as was Joseph Smith. He was loved of the Lord in the premortal life, as was Joseph Smith, and he was chosen there for his mortal career, just as was our modern prophet.

The scriptures reveal that before the world was made, there was a war in heaven:

''And there was war in heaven: Michael and his angels fought against the dragon; and the dragon fought and his angels,

''And prevailed not; neither was their place found any more in heaven.

''And the great dragon was cast out, that old serpent, called the Devil, and Satan, which deceiveth the whole world: he was cast out into the earth, and his angels were cast out with him.'' (Revelation 12:7-9.)

John further wrote of this Satan: ''And it was given unto him to make war with the saints, and to overcome them: and power was given him over all kindreds, and tongues, and nations. And all that dwell upon the earth shall worship him, whose names are not written in the book of life of the Lamb slain from the foundation of the world. If any man have an ear, let him hear.'' (Revelation 13:7-9.)

Satan was able to sway a third of the hosts of heaven who were willing to join his rebellion.

It seems reasonable to believe that there must have been many spirits who were less valiant. But for the faithful in that pristine period, a notable reward was in store. They were to be born in a lineage on earth with a divine promise and great opportunities. The Lord would provide for them a special progenitor, a man of God, and through his lineage they would receive the "believing blood" to help them accept the truth once they arrived in mortality.

Abraham—the friend of God even in the premortal life, one of the great ones, one of the leaders in the host of righteous spirits—was selected to be that progenitor. Through his posterity would all the peoples of the earth be blessed.

Although the Lord gave a special status to the preexistent faithful, he was not showing any unearned favoritism, for he is fair and just to all. Notably, he is no respecter of persons.

Abraham, by his faithfulness in the premortal life, earned the right to be the progenitor of the faithful spirits who themselves had earned the right to be born in that lineage.

They would not only be born in the "believing blood" line, but they would also become the ministers of the Lord in the mortal world. They would hold his priesthood; they would lead his church when it was established.

So the Lord was planning far ahead for us and for priesthood leaders to direct us. Neither birth nor death is a barrier to his work. He sees the overall from the eternal point of view and makes his plans accordingly.

But he did more than plan for his primeval faithful and their welfare when they arrived in mortality. He also was merciful to those who were not so faithful. He held out to them the opportunity to become believers. Here on earth they could acquire the necessary faith, if they would obey, and they could then return to the good graces of the Lord.

If they would accept his gospel on earth and would live it all the days of their lives, they would become heirs of the same blessings promised to those born in the line of faithful Abraham. Although they would be born of other lineage, they could still be blessed with faithful Abraham if only they would obey the Lord.

Says President Joseph Fielding Smith in his book *The Way to Perfection* (pp. 89-90):

"No person can receive the Gospel without becoming of the seed of Abraham. If they are not of his blood by descent they become so by adoption. . . . Moreover, the Lord revealed to Joseph Smith that all who receive the two Priesthoods become sons of Moses and of Aaron, and 'the seed of Abraham, and the church and kingdom, and the elect of God.' (D&C 84:33-48.) This is done by virtue of the covenant made with Abraham, which was renewed with Jacob and the tribes of Israel.''

President Smith further said:

"The covenant the Lord made with Abraham was of three-fold nature as a blessing to mankind to the latest generations. We do not fully comprehend its significance even now. Perhaps we will not until we enter celestial glory. The priesthood and its powers were to descend through Abraham's posterity. It was through him that Christ was to come, and thus prove a blessing to all nations. Moreover, the promise was made that in addition to Abraham's direct descendants, all who should receive the Gospel from that time forth, should also become of Abraham's seed by adoption, and his blood should be mixed among the nations to leaven them with the privileges of the Gospel.'' (Ibid., pp. 87-88.)

What a great testimony to the mercy of Almighty God!

Even those who were casual, even those who were careless in premortal life, will receive opportunity here on earth to receive the gospel and be saved if they will hearken fully to the word of God. Though they may be born in the lineage of other peoples, and not of Abraham, they may nevertheless still "join with Abraham" and be counted with his children.

Then who was Abraham? Can anyone properly measure his stature and his acceptance before God? He was indeed God's friend, his faithful servant, and now would become the foun-tainhead through whom all the nations of the earth would be blessed.

But more than that. Abraham was also chosen to become the mortal progenitor of the line in which Jesus the Christ would come to earth. It would be through Abraham's lineage that Jesus would be born at Bethlehem!

Was not he a chosen vessel? Was not God his friend?

Chapter 10

UR OF THE CHALDEES

Abraham, or Abram, as he was first called, was born in Ur of the Chaldees, one of the most important of the ancient cities in southern Mesopotamia. He was the tenth generation from Noah.

Ur was a city of about a half million population in the time of Abraham, according to archaeologists. It was given over to wickedness and idolatry. Yet it had beautiful buildings, good schools, and extensive business dealings by sea as well as on land. The remains of some of the docks are still discernible in the harbor.

The site has been excavated for years by archaeologists. It is located 140 miles south of Babylon, about ten miles from the present bed of the Euphrates. In all likelihood the city was built originally on the banks of that river.

About a mile and a half from the excavation site is a modern junction of the Baghdad Railway in southern Iraq, known as the Ur Junction.

The main excavations were made shortly after the end of World War I through the joint sponsorship of the British Museum of London and the Department of Archaeology at the University of Pennsylvania. Most of the work was done under Sir Leonard Woolley between 1922 and 1934. Extensive finds were made there, illustrating almost every period of the city's history.

It is believed that Ur was founded some time in the fourth millennium B.C. Excavators say that their evidence indicates that it was wiped out by the flood of Noah's day, but that following the deluge, the city was rebuilt.

Ur became the capital of the entire Mesopotamian valley under the reign of the Sumerian kings (2700 B.C.). Cemetery excavations have produced "almost incredible treasures in gold, silver, bronze and semi-precious stones," indicating not only wealth but also a high degree of civilization. Some inscriptions

corroborate the existence of the fabled Sargon of Akkad (2400
B.C.).

In the period beginning with 2100 B.C., stepped pyramids
were built there for the worship of the moon god. Sumerian ar-
chitects, as early as 2600 B.C., were familiar with the arch, the
column, the vault, the dome, and other basic forms of architec-
ture.

There is evidence of extensive commerce by ocean-going
vessels between Ur and the Far East, with traffic in gold, silver,
ivory, and hard wood. Many clay tablets were found that reveal
these facts.

Homes were generally of the two-story type, much like the
Arab houses in Baghdad. The well-to-do had homes large
enough to provide guest rooms, servants' quarters, and lounging
areas, yet with adequate privacy.

Little chapels or shrines to the moon god were built at the rear
of most houses of the wealthy class; these were used also for
numerous family gods and other minor deities. The dead in the
families were usually buried under the floors of either these
chapels or the private homes.

An irrigation system was developed at Ur, as well as in
nearby areas, for in this arid country farming depended almost
entirely on the Euphrates River. This source of irrigation water
was abundant and brought great productivity to the area. In about
400 B.C., for some reason the river changed its course and reduced
that entire area to a desert, since the irrigation system could no
longer function.

In the *New Catholic Encyclopedia* we read:

"The archaeological evidence shows that Ur was first occupied by settlers (perhaps pre-Sumerians) who, during the
Chalcolithic Age (*c*. 4000-3000), adapted the so-called Obeidian
culture of *c*. 3700 (named after Obeid, a site near Ur), which is
found also at Uruk, Lagash, Eridu, and other places. By the
Warka (*c*. 3200) and Jemdet Nasr (*c*. 3000) Periods, Ur was certainly inhabited by Sumerians.

"Apparently from the Early Dynastic Period I (*c*. 2900-
2700) come the famous so-called Royal Tombs of Ur with their
wealth of jewelry and magnificent works of art. In the tomb of the
lady Shub-ad, 74 of her courtiers or servants (68 of them women)

were buried with her—the only know occurrence of such mass burials in ancient Mesopotamia. . . .

"... the city reached the zenith of its glory in the Third Dynasty of Ur (*c.* 2060-1950), when, under its Kings Urnammu, Shulgi, and their three successors, immense temples were built, and the closely packed dwellings, which must have housed more than one-half million people, covered an area of about 4 square miles." (New York: McGraw Hill, 1967, 14:476.)

In the excavations, not only are items of monetary value found, but also evidence of the culture of the city. Among the discoveries are clay tablets bearing mathematical square and cube-root computations, word lists in Sumerian, temple receipts for tithes and taxes, and business records demonstrating the extensive nature of Ur's commerce.

The Biblical World, a dictionary of biblical archaeology, says the following:

"Many other discoveries related directly to the burial practices of the early Sumerians. There was much evidence of servants and attendants being buried alive with the rulers. In one tomb at least sixty-eight court women and six other servants joined their ruler in death. The quiet repose of the attendants suggests that they were either drugged before being placed in the tomb or voluntarily took sleeping potions. Soldiers with spears, musicians with costly harps, and servants with the royal ox cart paid the supreme price." (Charles F. Pfeiffer, ed., New York: Bonanza Books, 1966, pp. 601-2.)

This same authority raises some question about the actual location of Ur, as to whether it was in southern Mesopotamia or in the north, near Haran.

C. H. Gordon, renowned archaeologist and scholar, also raises the same question. It is thought by some that Urfa, a town twenty miles northwest of Haran, might possibly have been Ur. Gordon prefers to regard Ur as the town of Ura, a Hittite city, north and east of Haran.

In any case, whether in the north or in the south, the site was nevertheless in Mesopotamia. It was still "Ur of the Chaldees," as Abraham called his original home.

J. O. Kinnaman (A.B., A.M., Ph.D., D.D.), in his book

Diggers for Facts, says that in the time of Abraham, Ur had ceased to be of major political importance but had become a center of pagan religion and culture. It had city museums, libraries, good schools "and all the refinements known to human society."

Dr. Kinnaman claims that Ur was a city before the flood, and was rebuilt after Noah's time. He says further that "the art of writing is as old as the [human] race. It came into the world with them, and has never been lost since. This art was very old when Abraham went to school. In fact, it was so old that the Sumerian, at the time of Abraham, was a dead language just as Latin and Classical Greek are today." He also says that "there was absolutely no illiteracy in Ur in the time of Abraham." (Haverhill, Mass.: Destiny Publishers, 1940, pp. 64, 67.)

Hammurabi was the ruler of the area in Abraham's day, it is said, and he was a patron of schools, learning, and the arts.

Dr. Kinnaman speaks of business contracts written in cuneiform being found on clay tablets. He writes of one such: "The name signed by the party of the first part is the same as that scratched on the wall beside the door casing of the house— ABRAM. . . . Let me say that of the hundreds upon hundreds of thousands of tablets discovered and translated, this is the only one with the name, ABRAM." (Ibid., p. 71.) This account is not confirmed by other archaeologists.

ABRAHAM'S EARLY LIFE

If the conflict between Isaac and Ishmael, Hagar and Sarah, caused Abraham concern, it was not the first time that family strife had invaded his home.

In his early life in Ur, there was even more serious trouble than that which arose over Ishmael. Abraham apparently grew up in a home that at first consisted of believers in the true God. Later, apostasy invaded the family, and this brought on the conflict.

Abraham was obviously a well-educated man. His family was small, but is considered by archaeologists to have been fairly well off. He lived with his father, Terah, who vacillated between idolatry and true religion.

Terah had three sons, Abram, Nahor, and Haran. Haran had two daughters who are mentioned in the Bible. One was Iscah, about whom nothing more is said. The other was Milcah, who became the wife of Nahor, Abraham's brother. Haran also had a son named Lot, with whom Abraham had many dealings.

The record says that "Terah lived seventy years and begat Abram, Nahor and Haran."

Abraham must have been taught the true gospel in his youth, even though his father and other members of the family later apostatized. When his home became an open invitation for him to adopt idolatry, he did not yield. He remained true and faithful to the gospel teachings.

It is not known how he obtained the record of his fathers, but that record certainly provided him with information concerning the priesthood and its many blessings, instilling in him a strong desire to be ordained to that priesthood.

Because of Abraham's great faithfulness, the Lord gave him the Urim and Thummim. It was a source of many revelations, which further established him in the faith by teaching him concerning the true God, as contrasted with the gods of wood and stone worshipped by his father. His possession of that instrument and his own desire to live the gospel apparently prompted him to try to reconvert his family and bring them back to the true faith. But they resisted completely.

In those days Mesopotamia was engulfed in idolatry. It was the popular thing. Those who opposed it were condemned as human sacrifices on the altars of the heathen gods. Religions of the nearby nations apparently were mixed with those of the natives of Ur. Abraham spoke of several gods as he described the heathen loyalties of his family and said:

"My fathers having turned from their righteousness, and from the holy commandments which the Lord their God had given unto them, unto the worshiping of the gods of the heathen, utterly refused to hearken to my voice;

"For their hearts were set to do evil, and were wholly turned to the god of Elkenah, and the god of Libnah, and the god of Mahmackrah, and the god of Korash, and the god of Pharaoh, king of Egypt;

"Therefore they turned their hearts to the sacrifice of the heathen in offering up their children unto their dumb idols, and hearkened not unto my voice, but endeavored to take away my life by the hand of the priest of Elkenah. The priest of Elkenah was also the priest of Pharaoh." (Abraham 1:5-7.)

He explained further that these deities required human sacrifices. Particularly was this true of the religion evidently imported from Egypt. Of it he said:

"Now, at this time it was the custom of the priest of Pharaoh, the king of Egypt, to offer up upon the altar which was built in the land of Chaldea, for the offering unto these strange gods, men, women, and children.

"And it came to pass that the priest made an offering unto the god of Pharaoh, and also unto the god of Shagreel, even after the manner of the Egyptians. Now the god of Shagreel was the sun.

"Even the thank-offering of a child did the priest of Pharaoh offer upon the altar which stood by the hill called Potiphar's Hill, at the head of the plain of Olishem." (Abraham 1:8-10.)

Abraham here not only spoke of the local gods of Ur, but also of the Egyptian gods. He mentions that the priest of Elkenah was also the priest of Pharaoh. The altar was obviously specially built for human sacrifice.

How did this Egyptian infusion reach into Mesopotamia? What was the priest of Pharaoh doing in Ur?

At this time Egyptian influence was felt throughout the Fertile Crescent. Much of the advanced learning of the people of the Nile was exported abroad, including some of their religious customs. For example, a powerful bow that would shoot an arrow straight for a distance of 1,000 to 1,400 feet was invented in Egypt, and it became a major weapon used by the entire region.

Furthermore, even prior to 3000 B.C. the Egyptians had developed an alphabet, the earliest known to historians. This was borrowed by other nations, together with writing materials. The Egyptians found that they could make an excellent ink by mixing water with a little vegetable gum and then stirring it in soot from their blackened pots. A pointed reed, dipped into the mixture, made a usable pen. This too was adopted in nearby nations.

The Egyptians developed the use of papyrus, which was made from river reed. The papyrus was cut into strips and glued together, thus making paper of whatever size was desired. This stimulated writing and greatly facilitated record keeping in neighboring countries. It was far more convenient than the use of clay tablets.

In the same manner the religions of the Egyptians were also exported to nearby peoples. Hence there were priests of Pharaoh in Ur.

But as a young man, Abraham loved the Lord. "I sought for mine appointment unto the Priesthood according to the appointment of God unto the fathers," he wrote. He added: "Finding there was greater happiness and peace and rest for me, I sought for the blessings of the fathers, and the right whereunto I should be ordained to administer the same." (Abraham 1:4, 2.)

It was this desire and his innate righteousness that led to his decision to leave Ur. But God also commanded it, and Abraham obeyed. "In the land of the Chaldeans, at the residence of my father, I, Abraham, saw that it was needful for me to obtain another place of residence." (Abraham 1:1.)

It would be interesting to know how a knowledge of the fathers reached Ur originally, and how Abraham obtained their records, but concerning this, both history and scripture are silent. It is revealed, as has been said, that he had the Urim and Thummim.

The fact that Abraham had the records of the fathers is most interesting though. Of this he wrote: "But the records of the fathers, even the patriarchs, concerning the right of Priesthood, the Lord my God preserved in mine own hands; therefore a knowledge of the beginning of the creation, and also of the planets, and of the stars, as they were made known unto the fathers, have I kept even unto this day, and I shall endeavor to write some of these things upon this record, for the benefit of my posterity that shall come after me." (Abraham 1:31.)

It is notable that these records contained information about the stars and the planets. What an insight this gives concerning the "fathers"! How had they learned astronomy? Did God teach them in the days of their righteousness as he later taught both Abraham and Moses? In further revelations Abraham personally obtained additional knowledge about the structure of the heavens and details concerning the creation of this earth.

Had there been a strong branch of the church in Mesopotamia, and had its membership later been swallowed up in the idolatry of their neighbors, leaving Abraham alone in the faith?

His father at one time was a believer. Were his grandfather, and possibly his great-grandfather also believers? The little that we do know seems to indicate that the knowledge of God—and the priesthood—had been handed down through the generations. But how did those generations get over into Ur?

Of course, the tendency in those days, as it is today, was for the people to travel to various parts of the country. It began with the tower of Babel. It is not at all unreasonable to suppose that some of the faithful drifted over to Mesopotamia. Certainly there is much evidence that early civilizations developed and thrived in that area. Some historians call Mesopotamia the cradle of civilization.

A branch of "the fathers" could have developed there and left their records undisturbed when they apostatized. Through his faithfulness, Abraham understood the value of those records, appreciated them, and sought to obtain the blessings that the gospel had offered to the fathers.

The Prophet Joseph Smith made this interesting comment:

"It will be noticed that, according to Paul, (see Gal. iii:8) the Gospel was preached to Abraham. We would like to be informed in what name the Gospel was then preached, whether it was in the name of Christ or some other name. If in any other name, was it the Gospel? And if it was the Gospel, and that preached in the name of Christ, had it any ordinances? If not, was it the Gospel? And if it had ordinances what were they?

"Our friends may say, perhaps, that there were never any ordinances except those of offering sacrifices before the coming of Christ, and that it could not be possible for the Gospel to have been administered while the law of sacrifices of blood was in force.

"But we will recollect that Abraham offered sacrifice, and notwithstanding this, had the Gospel preached to him. That the offering of sacrifice was only to point the mind forward to Christ, we infer from these remarkable words of Jesus to the Jews: 'Your father Abraham rejoiced to see my day: and he saw it, and was glad' (John viii:56).

"So, then, because the ancients offered sacrifice it did not hinder their hearing the Gospel; but served, as we said before, to open their eyes, and enable them to look forward to the time of the coming of the Savior, and rejoice in His redemption.

"We find also, that when the Israelites came out of Egypt they had the Gospel preached to them, according to Paul in his letter to the Hebrews, which says: 'For unto us was the gospel preached, as well as unto them: but the word preached did not profit them, not being mixed with faith in them that heard it.' (See Heb. iv:2).

"It is said again, in Gal. iii:19, that the law (of Moses, or the Levitical law) was 'added' because of transgression. What, we ask, was this law added to, if it was not added to the Gospel? It must be plain that it was added to the Gospel, since we learn that they had the Gospel preached to them.

"From these few facts, we conclude that whenever the Lord revealed Himself to men in ancient days, and commanded them to offer sacrifice to Him, that it was done that they might look forward in faith to the time of His coming, and rely upon the power of that atonement for a remission of their sins.

"And this they have done, thousands who have gone before us, whose garments are spotless, and who are, like Job, waiting with an assurance like his, that they will see Him in the *latter day* upon the earth, even in their flesh." (HC 2:17.)

As an illustration of the fact that the church was well-established in Abraham's day, we quote the following from Helaman in the Book of Mormon:

"And now behold, Moses did not only testify of these things, but also all the holy prophets, from his days even to the days of Abraham.

"Yea, and behold I say unto you, that Abraham not only knew of these things, but there were many before the days of Abraham who were called by the order of God; yea, even after the order of his Son; and this that it should be shown unto the people, a great many thousand years before his coming, that even redemption should come unto them." (Helaman 8:16, 18.)

Prior to the birth of Christ the Nephites had both the gospel and the law of Moses, and they observed both.

Chapter 12

ABRAHAM ATTACKED

Abraham's intense loyalty to the true God and his efforts to help his relatives to repent of their idolatry brought on a severe family feud. Particularly was Terah, his father, disturbed. His concern went to the point where he sought the death of Abraham. Why would this be? Why would a father seek to destroy his own son?

It would seem that Terah was so distressed over Abraham's opposition to idolatry; he was so desirous that Abraham be forgiven of his attitude by the pagan god that he sought some kind of appeasement on behalf of his son.

Terah was a devotee of a religion that demanded human sacrifice as appeasement. He was a sun worshipper. The priest of the cult of the "god of Pharaoh" was also the priest of the sun god Shagreel. (Abraham 1:9.)

Abraham's father and others of his relatives "endeavored to take away my life by the hand of the priest of Elkenah," said Abraham in his own account. (Abraham 1:7.) That could mean only one thing: The family intended to have Abraham sacrificed on the altar to appease the sun god. In Abraham 1:30 Abraham again speaks of Terah's desire to take away his life.

Did Terah believe so much in the sun god that he would seek to placate that deity by sacrificing Abraham to him? The heathen priest already had sacrificed three young women on this same altar because they would not yield their virtue and refused to "bow down to worship gods of wood or of stone, therefore they were killed upon this altar, and it was done after the manner of the Egyptians." (Abraham 1:11.)

It seemed to be Terah's intention to provide the same treatment for his son. It does not appear that there was any desire on his part to murder Abraham in a fit of anger because of a family quarrel. It seems more likely that it was a sacrifice of atonement that Terah sought, probably out of his fatherly love for his son.

He may have thought that this extreme method should be used to save Abraham's soul. That at least is the charitable point of view, and most likely the correct one.

In the legends of both Jews and Arabs is a story that says that Abraham destroyed his father's images, and that this so infuriated the "god-king" Nimrod that he had Abraham thrown into a fiery furnace, only to be rescued immediately by the angel Gabriel.

That Abraham strongly fought idolatry is an accepted fact. That his attitude gave his father great concern is also beyond question.

Other parents offered their little children and sometimes their older children, or even grown men and women, as peace offerings to these gods. Why not Terah? Would Abraham's death appease Shagreel? In any case, "it came to pass that the priests laid violence upon me, that they might slay me also, as they did those virgins upon this altar." (Abraham 1:12.)

Abraham must have resisted this attack, but he was overpowered. However, he wrote, as the priests "lifted up their hands upon me, that they might offer me up and take away my life, behold, I lifted up my voice unto the Lord my God, and the Lord hearkened and heard, and he filled me with the vision of the Almighty, and the angel of his presence stood by me, and immediately unloosed my bands;

"And his voice was unto me: Abraham, Abraham, behold, my name is Jehovah, and I have heard thee, and have come down to deliver thee, and to take thee away from thy father's house, and from all thy kins-folk, into a strange land which thou knowest not of;

"And this because they have turned their hearts away from me, to worship the god of Elkenah, and the god of Libnah, and the god of Mahmackrah, and the god of Korash, and the god of Pharaoh, king of Egypt; therefore I have come down to visit them, and to destroy him who hath lifted up his hand against thee, Abraham, my son, to take away thy life." (Abraham 1:15-17.)

The Lord broke down the altars of Elkenah and the other gods and smote the priest "that he died."

When the scripture says that the Lord broke down the altars of the gods of the land, it must have had broad repercussions because it brought great mourning in Chaldea "and also in the court of Pharaoh." Pharaoh and his court were in Egypt. Only a most unusual event could have caused such extensive and distant reactions.

Abraham's brief account obviously does not tell the whole story. Abraham wrote that this attack took place on Potiphar's Hill in the land of Ur of Chaldea. The record also says that Potiphar's Hill was at the head of the plain of Olishem. (V. 10.)

The hill in Ur called after Potiphar reminds us of Joseph who was sold into Egypt, where he became the servant of Potiphar, a captain of the Egyptian guard. (Genesis 39:1.) The Bible dictionary says that the name Potiphar signifies "belonging to the sun." Hence it was related to sun worship.

But what of the name Olishem? Could it be divided into Oli-Shem, and did it refer in some way to Shem, the righteous son of Noah?

We next read this:

"Now, after the priest of Elkenah was smitten that he died, there came a fulfilment of those things which were said unto me concerning the land of Chaldea, that there should be a famine in the land.

"Accordingly a famine prevailed throughout all the land of Chaldea, and my father was sorely tormented because of the famine, and he repented of the evil which he had determined against me, to take away my life." (Abraham 1:29-30.)

So severe was the famine that Haran, the brother of Abraham, died there in Ur. Terah "was sorely tormented because of the famine" (v. 30), and no doubt when Haran died, Terah was even further softened in his heart, helping to bring about repentance.

The time for Abraham's removal from Ur had now arrived. "Now the Lord had said unto me: Abraham, get thee out of thy country, and from thy kindred, and from thy father's house, unto a land that I will show thee." (Abraham 2:3.)

Abraham prepared to go. First he married Sarah. Nahor, his brother, married Milcah, daughter of Haran.

Nahor did not leave Ur with Abraham, but seems to have moved to Haran later on. Nothing is said about any other relatives but Abraham's nephew Lot.

Except for Sarah, Lot, and Terah, who "followed along" somewhat repentant, Abraham was alone. And so we read: "Therefore I left the land of Ur, of the Chaldees, to go into the land of Canaan; and I took Lot, my brother's son, and his wife, and Sarai my wife; and also my father followed after me, unto the land which we denominated Haran." (Abraham 2:4.)

On the way to Canaan they rested in northern Mesopotamia in a place that they named Haran, after the dead brother of Abraham. There the famine abated. With the return of prosperity, Terah went back to his idolatry. Not wishing to continue with Abraham to the promised land, he remained in Haran and subsequently died at the age of 205 years. (Genesis 11:32.) This was approximately 1921 B.C.

The region of Haran has other interests also. Bible dictionaries say that Nahor, who did not accompany Abraham on his journey north, afterward went to Haran to live, no doubt to be with his father and any other relatives who may have gathered there.

Nahor's son Bethuel became the father of Rebeccah, who married Isaac, Abraham's son. Bethuel also had a son named Laban, who had two daughters, Rachel and Leah. They became the wives of Jacob, Abraham's grandson.

Haran is in the area that later was known as Paddan-aram. Aram is an alternate name for Syria. Haran was located north and east of Palestine.

Chapter 13

THE DIVINE CALL

The altar of Elkenah was more than a heathen shrine to Abraham, and far more than the place where he nearly lost his life. It was where he received his divine call!

While the priests of Pharoah "lifted up their hands" to take his life, he prayed earnestly to the Lord for deliverance. "And the Lord hearkened and heard, and he filled me with the vision of the Almighty, and the angel of his presence stood by me, and immediately unloosed my bands." That was the first step in the miracle.

Next came the voice of the Lord, saying, "Abraham, Abraham, behold, my name is Jehovah, and I have heard thee, and have come down to deliver thee, and to take thee away from thy father's house, and from all thy kins-folk, into a strange land which thou knowest not of." (Abraham 1:15-16.)

Note the reference to the relatives of Abraham: "all thy kins-folk." What a tragedy that the whole family fell away from the faith, making it necessary for the Lord to uproot Abraham, take him away entirely, and lead him to a strange land "which thou knowest not of."

That last expression is interesting, too. He was to go to Palestine. Apparently that land was not known to him personally. Communication in those days, of course, was limited. But there was frequent contact between Egypt and Mesopotamia otherwise, and the travel route went through Palestine. Obviously Abraham had never been there or learned of it, or the Lord would not have spoken as he did.

There must have been at least two sections of the Lord's church in those days. One in Ur ended in apostasy, with Abraham leaving to seek a better land. The other was certainly in Palestine, for there we know Melchizedek lived. He was the great high priest, and to him Abraham paid tithes. He also was the king of the city of Salem, believed to be ancient Jerusalem.

It is firmly stated that some of the fathers lived in Ur, for they apparently prepared or possessed the record that fell into Abraham's hands. Those fathers very likely held the priesthood, giving Abraham a desire for the same blessing.

How these fathers got over into Mesopotamia can only be surmised. People moved about in those days as they do today. At the tower of Babel they were scattered far and wide. Archaeologists tell us that Mesopotamia cradled the first civilization.

But the church must have been a going concern in those days, especially since it had such a great high priest as Melchizedek. His greatness must be measured by the fact that the priesthood after the order of the Son of God was named after him to avoid the too frequent use of the name of Deity. What other man ever received such an honor?

Paul knew that the church existed then, for he told the Galatians (3:8) that the gospel was preached "before unto Abraham."

The Book of Mormon clearly says that Melchizedek lived in Salem, where he was king.

Peloubet's *Bible Dictionary* (p. 577) says of Salem's location: "No satisfactory identification of it is perhaps possible. Two main opinions have been current from the earliest ages of interpretation: (a) That of the Jewish commentators, who affirm that Salem is Jerusalem, on the ground that Jerusalem is so called in Psalms 76:2. Nearly all Jewish commentators hold this opinion, and also the majority of the best modern scholars. (b) Jerome, however, states that the Salem of Melchizedek [is identified] with Salim, near Aenon, where John baptized."

The psalm referred to reads: "In Judah is God known: his name is great in Israel. In Salem also is his tabernacle, and his dwelling place in Zion." (Psalm 76:1-2.)

Regardless of which is correct, Salem in any case was in Palestine, and there King Melchizedek reigned. He and Abraham were contemporaries.

No doubt a knowledge of the church in Palestine at that time was kept from Abraham in Ur by his immediate fathers, since they had turned to wickedness. They apparently shut out of their minds and lives everything pertaining to the true faith.

Since Abraham's fathers had been in possession of the records that later fell into his hands, surely they must have had more knowledge than they had imparted to Abraham about the "strange land which thou knowest not of."

While Abraham was lying on the sacrificial altar, an angel came and saved him from the knife of Pharoah's priest. And there Abraham received his call.

"Behold," said the Lord at this dreadful moment, as he killed the priest and destroyed the altar, "I will lead thee by the hand, and I will take thee, to put upon thee my name, even the Priesthood of thy father, and my power shall be over thee.

"As it was with Noah so shall it be with thee; but through thy ministry my name shall be known in the earth forever, for I am thy God." (Abraham 1:18-19.)

These are interesting scriptures. It was later that Abraham was told of his great posterity, but here he was called to take upon himself the ministry and the name of Jehovah, who is Jesus Christ. At the heathen altar also he was promised the priesthood and was told, "my power shall be with thee."

Here too he was told the name of Jehovah, who said: "I am thy God."

We often speculate about the extent of the Lord's subsequent promise of a vast posterity, but here is a promise that is seldom mentioned: "Through thy ministry my name shall be known in the earth forever." (Abraham 1:19.)

This mighty prophet of God would not be left merely to propagate a great posterity. A ministry was given him! It must have included the preaching of the word. But to what congregations? The record is silent on this point. We do know that he taught the Egyptians astronomy. Could he have used that as a means of proclaiming the name of Christ in that spiritually benighted land?

And surely if there were sufficient members of the Church in Palestine to justify having a "great high priest," there would have been congregations for Abraham to address. It is remembered that when Melchizedek preached repentance to his own people, he converted his entire city. (Alma 13:7-18.) Since he and Abraham were contemporaries and both were called of God, would they not have been associated together in the ministry?

One means by which Abraham declares the name of Jehovah to all the world is through the generations of the Jews themselves.

Believing Jews are loyal to Abraham and to their heritage through him. They cherish Jehovah's name. Inasmuch as they were scattered among all nations, they took the name of Jehovah and the memory of Abraham with them, universally.

But Jehovah is also Jesus Christ, and with his name true Christians also carry the name of Abraham worldwide in their ministry. Latter-day Saints in particular do so. They are now in seventy nations, and as they preach Christ they also carry with them the name of Abraham, in whose lineage Jesus was born.

After his escape from the priest of Pharaoh, Abraham was commanded to leave Ur. It was at this point that the Lord said: "Abraham, get thee out of thy country, and from thy kindred, and from thy father's house, unto a land that I will show thee." (Abraham 2:3.)

So he left Ur and went to Haran. There, he says, "the Lord appeared unto me, and said unto me: Arise, and take Lot with thee; for I have purposed to take thee away out of Haran, and to make of thee a minister to bear my name in a strange land which I will give unto thy seed after thee for an everlasting possession, when they hearken to my voice.

"For I am the Lord thy God; I dwell in heaven; the earth is my footstool; I stretch my hand over the sea, and it obeys my voice; I cause the wind and the fire to be my chariot; I say to the mountains—Depart hence—and behold, they are taken away by a whirlwind, in an instant, suddenly.

"My name is Jehovah, and I know the end from the beginning; therefore my hand shall be over thee.

"And I will make of thee a great nation, and I will bless thee above measure, and make thy name great among all nations, and thou shalt be a blessing unto thy seed after thee, that in their hands they shall bear this ministry and Priesthood unto all nations;

"And I will bless them through thy name; for as many as receive this Gospel shall be called after thy name, and shall be accounted thy seed, and shall rise up and bless thee, as their father;

"And I will bless them that bless thee, and curse them that curse thee; and in thee (that is, in thy Priesthood) and in thy seed (that is, thy Priesthood), for I give unto thee a promise that this right shall continue in thee, and in thy seed after thee (that is to say, the literal seed, or the seed of the body) shall all the families of the earth be blessed, even with the blessings of the Gospel, which are the blessings of salvation, even of life eternal.'' (Abraham 2:6-11.)

This was the call of Abraham. This was his blessing. And his work was indeed a ministry!

Chapter 14

THE HEAVENLY PROMISE

The promise of the Lord to Abraham, that through his lineage all the nations of the earth would be blessed, is most significant.

It will be remembered that Abraham was shown in vision the premortal spirits, the mighty ones. He was told by the Lord that ''these I will make my rulers; . . . Abraham, thou art one of them; thou wast chosen before thou wast born.'' (Abraham 3:22-23.)

He was chosen in that pristine period for the blessing that the Lord now pronounced upon him. In the spirit world were many chosen and loyal spirits who were blessed to come into mortality through the loins of Abraham, who also was blessed in being chosen as their progenitor. The Lord thus was to send his most loyal spirits to be born in a lineage that would encourage the worship of Jehovah and help to prepare them to receive and minister in the holy priesthood.

The promise is usually spoken of as being twofold:

1. Jesus was to be born in his lineage. Salvation is offered to all men through faith in Christ. Resurrection comes to all human beings through him, whether they believe in him or not.

2. The blood of Israel, through the scattering of the tribes, was sprinkled among all nations, thus distributing the ''believing blood'' everywhere. This provides for all mankind an additional opportunity to believe the words of the Good Shepherd and to recognize his voice when they hear it.

President Joseph Fielding Smith explained it this way:

''How were the nations benefited by the covenant made with Abraham?

''First let us take a view of conditions before the flood. The Lord taught Adam the gospel after he was driven out of the Garden of Eden, and the Lord commanded him to teach his children.

''This Adam did, but we read that Satan came among them saying: 'I am also a son of God; and he commanded them, saying:

Believe it not; and they believed it not, and they loved Satan more than God. And men began from that time forth to be carnal, sensual, and devilish.' [Moses 5:13.]

"Therefore in the course of about sixteen hundred years the world had become corrupt and the Lord brought upon it the flood and cleansed it from its iniquity. With Noah and his family a new start was made, and the same commandments were given, and the people began to multiply and spread out over the earth.

"Like the antediluvians they too soon forgot the commandments of the Lord and turned to wickedness and idolatry. Therefore the Lord chose Abraham and commanded him to leave his native land and made a covenant with him that through his seed he would bless the world with the gospel. . . .

"It was to be by scattering the children of Israel among the nations of the earth that the Lord would bless them and make them entitled to the blessings of the gospel. The Lord took measures for this scattering soon after the Israelites entered the land of Palestine and had received their inheritances. . . .Evidence of the mixing of the seed of Israel among the gentile nations is shown at the time of the feast of Pentecost when Peter and the apostles addressed the assembly of Hebrews who had come to that feast, 'devout men, out of every nation under heaven.' [Acts 2:5.]

"These people evidently had been born in these foreign lands for they could not speak the language of the apostles and were astonished that each heard them in his own tongue. . . .

"One of the most interesting and significant parables ever written is that revealed to Zenos and recorded in the fifth chapter of Jacob in the Book of Mormon. It is a parable of the scattering of Israel. If we had the full key to the interpretation, then we would have in detail how Israel was transplanted in all parts of the earth.

"Thus through this scattering the Lord has caused Israel to mix with the nations and bring the gentiles within the blessings of the seed of Abraham. We are preaching the gospel now in all parts of the world, and for what purpose? To gather out from the gentile nations the lost sheep of the house of Israel. It is by this scattering that the gentile nations have been blessed, and if they will truly repent they are entitled to all the blessings promised to

Israel, 'which are the blessings of salvation, even of life eternal.' " (Improvement Era, February 1958, pp. 81, 116.)

Elder Orson F. Whitney of the Council of the Twelve, writing in the Liahona (*Elder's Journal*) June 17, 1924, spoke of it in this way:

"What was the purpose of Abraham's call? Why was he taken out of his own country and from his father's house and promised that he should become a great nation? It was because Mesopotamia was steeped in idolatry, and the time had arrived for the founding of a pure lineage through which the Lord Jesus Christ, the Savior, would come into the world. Abraham was required to separate himself from his idolatrous surroundings, that he might establish such a lineage. The strict laws given to Israel, Abraham's descendants, had as their object the preservation in purity of the lineage of our Lord, the 'Lamb without spot or blemish.' Isaiah, in the prophecy quoted, is exhorting latter-day Israel, scattered among all nations, but now being gathered out from all nations, to look unto Abraham, to remember the lineage from which they have sprung, and to prepare themselves for the great things that the Lord has in store for his people. . . .

"How was this great promise fulfilled? It was fulfilled in the coming of the Christ through the lineage of Abraham, Isaac and Jacob, to die for the redemption of a fallen world. It was also fulfilled in the fate that befell the House of Israel, who were dispersed among all nations for a wise purpose. . . .

"The Lord punished his people for their sins, just as he had punished Adam and Eve for their transgressions. But even as that was converted into a blessing—for the fall produced the human race—gave them bodies in the flesh—so the scattering of Israel, though a punishment upon the Lord's people for their disobedience was overruled to bring to pass in part the promise made to Abraham, that in his seed should all the nations of the earth be blessed.

"Prophecies of Israel's dispersion were made as early as the time of Moses, fifteen centuries before the birth of Christ. The great leader told his people, before they entered the Promised Land, that if they would serve Jehovah and keep his commandments, He would make of them a mighty nation, an independent nation; but if they forsook Jehovah and served other gods, He would scatter them from one end of the earth unto the other. Well, Israel did forsake Jehovah; they served other gods and polluted their noble lineage, by worshiping idols, by practicing the vices of the surrounding nations, making themselves temporarily unfit for the great mission unto which they had been called. And they had to be punished in order to be purified.''

Elder Whitney then referred to predictions that in the last days Israel would be gathered again. He asked: ''But why this gathering? What is it all about? What is the object in view? The house of Israel must be gathered because it is the God of Israel who is coming, and his people are the only people who have the right to prepare the way before him and meet him when he appears.

''It was the God of Israel who died to redeem the fallen human race, and it was the house of Israel, by its prophets and the Apostles, which prepared the way before Him and carried on the work that He began. God works through Israel in giving blessings to mankind. 'In thee (Abraham) and in thy seed shall all the nations of the earth be blessed.'

''We Latter-day Saints are Gentiles in part, but we have enough of the blood of Israel in our veins to recognize and appreciate the message that has come, and are not ashamed to stoop and pick up the diamond from the dust; for a diamond is a diamond, whether it sparkle in the dust at your feet or glitter in the diadem of a queen.

''God is coming to reign over the earth, to sanctify it and prepare it for eternal glory; for after it has passed away as by fire, it will be restored and converted into a celestial sphere. That is the destiny of our mother planet. It keeps the celestial law, wherefore it shall be sanctified and eventually glorified, as the abode of celestial beings. The King will come to Zion, a city to be built upon the North American continent, and then he will appear at Jerusalem, in the land of Palestine. . . .

''The work of gathering Ephraim and the other tribes will continue until it is complete. The kingdom of God throughout the Millennium will have two capital cities, Zion in America, Jerusalem in Palestine, and these words of Isaiah the prophet will then be fulfilled: 'Out of Zion shall go forth the law, and the word of the Lord from Jerusalem.' ''

Genealogies show Abraham to be directly related to various of the Eastern peoples. The *New Catholic Encyclopedia* (1:32-34) reports that through his brother Nehor, he is related to the Aramaeans, and that through his son Ishmael he is related to the Ishmaelites and to some branches of the Arab lines. He is related, of course, to Israel through Isaac and Jacob, and to the Edomites through Esau. Through his wife Keturah he is related to various Arabic tribes, and through his nephew Lot, to the Moabites and Ammonites.

Smith's Bible Dictionary (1:16) also mentions the Midianites as his relatives, and adds that his name was revered throughout Asia.

Chapter 15

ABRAHAM AND JOSEPH SMITH

The blessings and promises of Abraham were also conferred upon the Prophet Joseph Smith.

This was in harmony with the prediction of Peter that before the coming of the Savior there would be a restitution of all things whatsoever God had spoken by the mouth of all his holy prophets from the beginning of the world. (Acts 3:21.)

The Lord told the Prophet Joseph of an ancient personage named Esaias who received the priesthood under the hand of God. Where he resided is not mentioned. This Esaias lived in the days of Abraham "and was blessed of him." (D&C 84:12-13.)

This scripture established a definite relationship. A man who was so respected of the Lord that God himself would ordain him to the priesthood was associated with Abraham, who himself was the "friend of God." A friendship like that which existed between these two prophets, then, would seem to be most natural.

The revelation makes it clear that "Abraham received the priesthood from Melchizedek, who received it through the lineage of his fathers, even till Noah." (D&C 84:14.)

There can be no doubt in anyone's mind that the church was a progressive and ongoing institution at that time in Palestine. Further, the Lord appointed a "dispensation of the gospel" unto Abraham, and in it labored true prophets of Almighty God.

One of those prophets, Elias, had the keys of authority for that dispensation. As part of the restitution of all things spoken of by the apostle Peter, Elias came to Joseph Smith in the Kirtland Temple on April 3, 1836, and committed the keys of Abraham's dispensation to the modern restorer. In describing this event, Joseph and Oliver Cowdery said that "in us and our seed all generations after us should be blessed." (D&C 110:12.)

Remarkable, isn't it? This modern reconfirmation of the promise of Abraham was now bestowed upon Joseph Smith and

Oliver Cowdery, who were together in the temple at the time.

Naturally, of course, these keys and promises, like those bestowed through the coming of Moses and Elijah, related to the work of the entire church in these latter days, and were to be used by it.

This was part of the dispensation of the fulness of times, the rolling into one of all former dispensations, or a restoration of all things. Hence the coming of Elias to bestow the keys of Abraham's dispensation upon Joseph Smith. And hence the modern pronouncement of the Lord's promise to Abraham, this time extended to Joseph Smith and the Latter-day Saints.

When the Lord gave section 132 of the Doctrine and Covenants, he spoke of his covenant with Abraham and its relationship to Joseph Smith, the modern restorer of all things. Said he:

"I am the Lord thy God, and will give unto thee the law of my Holy Priesthood, as was ordained by me and my Father before the world was.

"Abraham received all things, whatsoever he received, by revelation and commandment, by my word, saith the Lord, and hath entered into his exaltation and sitteth upon his throne.

"Abraham received promises concerning his seed, and of the fruit of his loins—from whose loins ye are, namely, my servant Joseph—which were to continue so long as they were in the world; and as touching Abraham and his seed, out of the world they should continue; both in the world and out of the world should they continue as innumerable as the stars; or, if ye were to count the sand upon the seashore ye could not number them."

But then the Lord said: "This promise is *yours also*, because ye are of Abraham, and the promise was made unto Abraham; and by this law is the continuation of the works of my Father." (D&C 132:28-31. Italics added.)

When the construction of the Nauvoo House was under consideration, the Lord made this principle even more clear. Speaking of the Prophet Joseph Smith, the Lord said, "This anointing have I put upon his head, that his blessing shall also be put upon the head of his posterity after him.

"And as I said unto Abraham concerning the kindreds of the earth, even so I say unto my servant Joseph: In thee and in thy seed shall the kindred of the earth be blessed.

"Therefore, let my servant Joseph and his seed after him have place in that house, from generation to generation, forever and ever, saith the Lord.

"And let the name of that house be called Nauvoo House; and let it be a delightful habitation for man, and a resting-place for the weary traveler, that he may contemplate the glory of Zion, and the glory of this, the corner-stone thereof." (D&C 124:57-60.)

Thus, with the restoration of the gospel, the promises and blessings of Abraham were conferred as a part of the "restitution of all things, which God hath spoken by the mouth of all his holy prophets since the world began." (Acts 3:21. See also Matthew 25:31; 24:30; Ephesians 1:9; Revelation 14:6-7.)

Obviously there are great promises to Joseph Smith's posterity. If they will sustain the true church and be faithful, it appears that they will be heirs to the promises thus made to the Prophet and his seed.

This promise is also made to all Latter-day Saints, for we hold the priesthood with Joseph; we preach it abroad as he did and as he commanded. As children of Abraham and co-members of the Church with Joseph Smith, we bear Abraham's name abroad; we bear the Savior's name abroad, and gather in his— and Abraham's—people into the kingdom of God.

Abraham had the gospel of the Lord Jesus Christ and not some primitive belief. The gospel of salvation is what he had, and at this early time the destiny of his descendants to carry it abroad by the power of the priesthood was foretold. The promise mentioned no time limit, so was not that an early prediction of the work that we do today? Was there a time in the past—ever— when the gospel and the priesthood actually went to all nations? Was that work reserved for our day?

The Savior ministered only in Palestine. He commanded his disciples to go into all the world and preach the gospel to every nation, baptizing them in the name of the Lord. (Mark 16:15-16.)

But did they reach all nations? Little is known of their ministry, except that of Paul. But this we do know: As the early centuries passed, apostasy swept over the world, and what "all nations" eventually received was not the gospel of Christ, but a manmade version of it. And today, though so-called Christianity is worldwide, it is merely an apostate form of that gospel, with its many creeds and ordinances, and sometimes without any ordinances at all.

The scriptures indicate that it was to be in the latter days, through the restoration of the gospel, that the good word would be taken abroad universally as a warning before the second coming of the Lord. (Revelation 14:6-7; Acts 3:21.)

So we today, as Latter-day Saints, are even now helping to fulfill the promise made to Abraham that through him and his seed, both the gospel of salvation and the Holy Priesthood would be taken to all nations.

Chapter 16

GOD APPEARS IN PERSON

The personality of God is made clear through the repeated appearances of the Almighty to Abraham, who saw that the Lord was a person. Abraham talked with him face to face, as Moses did, or as do any two persons who commune together.

When Abraham was rescued from the pagan altar in Ur, the Lord spoke to him personally and said, "I . . . have come down to deliver thee." (Abraham 1:16.) The record does not say that he saw the Lord at this time.

But in Haran he did. "The Lord appeared to me," he said as the Lord commanded Abraham to leave Haran. "My name is Jehovah," the Lord continued in that conversation. And here he repeated his promise to Abraham. Then the patriarch writes: "Now, after the Lord had withdrawn from speaking to me, *and withdrawn his face from me. . . .*" (Abraham 2:12. Italics added.)

On the plains of Moreh when he offered sacrifices and prayed, he writes, "the Lord appeared unto me in answer to my prayers." (Abraham 2:19.) How close their relationship was! Truly Abraham was the Friend of God.

When he came near Egypt, the Lord directly addressed him again: "The Lord said unto me: Behold, Sarai, thy wife, is a very fair woman to look upon." (Abraham 2:22.)

It was direct communication—direct revelation!

When Abraham was shown the heavens by the use of the Urim and Thummim, he not only received revelations through that instrument, but he "talked with the Lord, *face to face*, as one man talketh with another; and he told me of the works which his hands had made.

"And he said unto me: My son, my son (and his hand was stretched out), behold I will show you all these." (Abraham 3:11-12. Italics added.)

Was not stretching out his hand a visual proof of the personality of God and of his being an individual, a person?

"He put his hand upon mine eyes," Abraham wrote. (Abraham 3:12.)

The revelation concerning astronomy included a personal visit and individual conversation between Abraham and the Lord—as "one man talketh to another." (Abraham 3:18-28.) What an experience to be thus taught of the Lord, and in his very presence!

The Lord spoke to Abraham in vision at other times. Then "when Abram was ninety years old and nine, the Lord appeared to Abram, and said unto him, I am the Almighty God; walk before me, and be thou perfect. And Abram fell on his face: and God talked with him." (Genesis 17:1, 3. See also Genesis 1:15.)

"And he left off talking with him, and God went up from Abraham." (Genesis 17:22.) "And the Lord appeared unto him in the plains of Mamre." (Genesis 18:1.)

When the angels visited with Abraham prior to the destruction of Sodom, the Lord was there too, for we read: "And the men turned their faces from thence, and went toward Sodom: but Abraham stood yet before the Lord." (Genesis 18:22.)

It was then that Abraham bargained with the Lord, evidently face to face, for the Lord had not yet left. He bargained for the righteous in the wicked cities of the plains. When the conversation was over we read that "the Lord went his way, as soon as he had left communing with Abraham: and Abraham returned unto his place." (Genesis 18:33.)

Such personal communications were the means by which the Friend of God visited with the Almighty.

There was no doubt in Abraham's mind that God is a person. There was no doubt in his mind that God is reasonable and can be approached, even talked with, face to face. There was no doubt about God's promises, and his fidelity, and his remembering his children and their needs.

God was a great reality to Abraham, and this fact Abraham taught to his children. So real was God to Isaac, for example, and so great was his faith that the Almighty also appeared to him.

It was this kind of association with God that set the foundation for the great religion that the patriarch passed on down to his descendants. In the house of Israel, there was full faith in a personal God.

Aside from the house of Israel, even among the illiterate and the savage, there always has been a certain conviction that God lives. In every human being there is an innate feeling that a Higher Power does indeed exist. It is on this spark of faith that they may build as they hear the true word of God, and learn the facts about both Abraham and God, but especially of themselves and their relationship with the Almighty.

God is a person! He is our eternal Father! He does live! We have the testimony of Abraham. We have the testimony of Christ. And in these latter days, it is reaffirmed through the Prophet Joseph Smith.

God does live!

Chapter 17

SARAH "THY SISTER"

The Lord would not allow Abraham to remain in Haran, even though his father stayed there and despite the fact that prosperity had come to him in that place. "So I, Abraham, departed as the Lord had said unto me, and Lot with me; and I, Abraham, was sixty and two years old when I departed out of Haran." (Abraham 2:14.)

They journeyed to Jershon where he made an altar and prayed to the Lord, asking that the famine might be turned "away from my father's house, that they might not perish."

As they reached the borders of Canaan, Abraham writes, "I offered sacrifice there in the plains of Moreh, and called on the Lord devoutly, because we had already come into the land of this idolatrous nation." Here again the Lord appeared to him, and again the Lord said—now in Canaan—"Unto thy seed will I give this land." (Abraham 2:17-19.)

Abraham continued to travel south. Canaan at that time was in famine also, and this persuaded him to go on to Egypt.

"And it came to pass when I was come near to enter into Egypt, the Lord said unto me: Behold, Sarai, thy wife, is a very fair woman to look upon;

"Therefore it shall come to pass, when the Egyptians shall see her, they will say—She is his wife; and they will kill you, but they will save her alive; therefore see that ye do on this wise:

"Let her say unto the Egyptians, she is thy sister, and thy soul shall live.

"And it came to pass that I, Abraham, told Sarai, my wife, all that the Lord had said unto me—Therefore say unto them, I pray thee, thou art my sister, that it may be well with me for thy sake, and my soul shall live because of thee." (Abraham 2:22-25.)

There was good reason for this. It was customary for the

kings and rulers to take to themselves any of the beautiful women their eyes fell upon. They had harems, of course, and did not mind adding to them.

Both the Bible and the Pearl of Great Price say that Sarah was a beauty. As she and Abraham came into Egypt, "the Egyptians beheld the woman that she was very fair. The princes also of Pharoah saw her, and commended her before Pharaoh." (Genesis 12:14-15.)

Pharaoh needed very little persuasion, and Sarah was soon taken into the king's house.

To protect himself, Abraham had told Pharaoh that Sarah was his sister, which of course she was. Had he divulged that she was his wife, he might have been slain. But as his sister, Pharaoh was willing to buy her at a good price. He offered Abraham "sheep, and oxen, and he asses, and menservants, and maidservants, and she asses, and camels." (Genesis 12:16.) All of this was the price he was willing to pay for Sarah.

The scripture does not mention the response of Abraham. Naturally he must have refused the offer because he was a man of God. In any case, it appears from the record that Sarah was detained in the king's house. This displeased the Lord, who knew that he would have to rescue her. He thereupon "plagued Pharaoh and his house with great plagues because of Sarai Abram's wife."

Through the plagues, the king apparently discovered the true relationship of Abraham and Sarah. As he wanted no more plagues on his house, he immediately lost all desire for Sarah. No woman was worth such a price.

He therefore called Abraham and said, "What is this that thou hast done unto me? why didst thou not tell me that she was thy wife? Why saidst thou, She is my sister? so I might have taken her to me to wife: now therefore behold thy wife, take her, and go thy way.

"And Pharaoh commanded his men concerning him: and they sent him away, and his wife, and all that he had." (Genesis 12:17-20.)

This, of course, was the result the Lord and Abraham both desired. They left in peace. The ruse succeeded, and Abraham was not slain by a Pharaoh lusting for just one more woman.

Abraham and Sarah had a second experience like this. When they journeyed to "the south country, and dwelled between Kadesh and Shur, and sojourned to Gerar," Abraham again said concerning Sarah, "She is my sister: and Abimelech king of Gerar sent, and took Sarah.

"But God came to Abimelech in a dream by night, and said to him, Behold, thou art but a dead man, for the woman which thou hast taken; for she is a man's wife.

"But Abimelech had not come near her: and he said, Lord, wilt thou slay also a righteous nation?

"Said he not unto me, She is my sister? and she, even she herself said, He is my brother: in the integrity of my heart and innocency of my hands have I done this.

"And God said unto him in a dream, Yea, I know that thou didst this in the integrity of thy heart; for I also withheld thee from sinning against me: therefore suffered I thee not to touch her.

"Now therefore restore the man his wife; for he is a prophet, and he shall pray for thee, and thou shalt live: and if thou restore her not, know thou that thou shalt surely die, thou, and all that are thine.

"Therefore Abimelech rose early in the morning, and called all his servants, and told all these things in their ears: and the men were sore afraid.

"Then Abimelech called Abraham, and said unto him, What hast thou done unto us? and what have I offended thee, that thou hast brought on me and on my kingdom a great sin? thou hast done deeds unto me that ought not to be done.

"And Abimelech said unto Abraham, What sawest thou, that thou hast done this thing?

"And Abraham said, Because I thought, Surely the fear of God is not in this place; and they will slay me for my wife's sake.

"And yet indeed she is my sister; she is the daughter of my father, but not the daughter of my mother; and she became my wife.

"And it came to pass, when God caused me to wander from my father's house, that I said unto her, This is thy kindness which thou shalt shew unto me; at every place whither we shall come, say of me, He is my brother.

"And Abimelech took sheep, and oxen, and menservants,

and womenservants, and gave them unto Abraham, and restored him Sarah his wife.

"And Abimelech said, Behold, my land is before thee: dwell where it pleaseth thee.

"And unto Sarah he said, Behold, I have given thy brother a thousand pieces of silver: behold, he is to thee a covering of the eyes, unto all that are with thee, and with all other: thus she was reproved.

"So Abraham prayed unto God: and God healed Abimelech, and his wife, and his maidservants; and they bare children.

"For the Lord had fast closed up all the wombs of the house of Abimelech, because of Sarah Abraham's wife." (Genesis 20:1-18.)

In both instances, the life of Abraham, as a husband to Sarah, was spared from lustful men. Sarah likewise was saved unhurt and untouched, and eventually she would achieve her own great destiny as the wife of Abraham. With him, she too would have progeny as numerous as the sands and the stars. And through her would be born even Jesus Christ, the Savior of all mankind.

Chapter 18

ABRAHAM WAS VERY RICH

No one really knows the economic condition of Abraham while he was in Ur as a young man. Archaeologists believe that he must have been well off and that most certainly he was well educated.

Nothing is said about his possessions as he moved to Haran. He evidently went with little of this world's goods. But in Haran he prospered. He says that in leaving Haran, he took his wife and nephew "and all our substance that we had gathered, and the souls that we had won in Haran." (Abraham 2:15.) The scriptures say that he obtained many servants. Actually at one time he had in his retinue three hundred armed and trained fighting men. (Genesis 14:14.) Another paragraph says: "There were many flocks in Haran." (Abraham 2:5.)

Susequent writings show that both Abraham and Lot had many herds, so many, in fact, that they found it necessary to part company to get more grazing land. Lot and his herds would go one way and Abraham with his would go another. Where did they obtain their herds?

There were several reasons why Abraham became rich. One must have been that he was a highly intelligent man, well educated in Ur, and trained no doubt in business as well as ranching. His business skill could have accounted for much of his successes, as it does with others. But there was a more important reason: He served the Lord!

When he said, "I will do well to hearken unto thy voice," he gave expression to a great lesson he had learned. This lesson was known also to the people of Lehi who came to America. They too were told that if they would serve God, they would be prospered in the land. This holds true of anyone, for the Lord is not a respecter of persons.

But learning to hearken unto the voice of the Lord included a great principle then, as it does now: the principle of tithing.

Abraham paid tithes of all he had to Melchizedek the great high priest. (Genesis 14:20.) Centuries later, when Malachi ministered for the Lord, he taught tithing with a great promise: "Bring ye all the tithes into the storehouse," he said. "Prove me now herewith, saith the Lord of hosts, if I will not open you the windows of heaven and pour you out a blessing that there shall not be room enough to receive it." (Malachi 3:8-10.)

Since Abraham had the gospel of Christ, he was, of course, taught this law. He certainly observed it. It is not supposed that paying tithing will make everyone rich, for other factors enter into it, but in any case the Lord does bless the faithful tithe payer.

As Abraham and Lot came up from Egypt, following the famine in Canaan and Haran, the record reads: "And Abram was very rich in cattle, in silver, and in gold. . . . And Lot also, which went [out of Egypt] with Abram had flocks and herds, and tents."

So it was that the land "was not able to bear them, that they might dwell together: for their substance was great, so that they could not dwell together.

"And there was a strife between the herdmen of Abram's cattle and the herdmen of Lot's cattle: and the Canaanite and the Perizzite dwelled then in the land.

"And Abram said unto Lot, Let there be no strife, I pray thee, between me and thee, and between my herdmen and thy herdmen; for we be brethren.

"Is not the whole land before thee? separate thyself, I pray thee, from me: if thou wilt take the left hand, then I will go to the right; or if thou depart to the right hand, then I will go to the left.

"And Lot lifted up his eyes, and beheld all the plain of Jordan, that it was well watered every where, before the Lord destroyed Sodom and Gomorrah, even as the garden of the Lord, like the land of Egypt, as thou comest unto Zoar.

"Then Lot chose him all the plain of Jordan; and Lot journeyed east: and they separated themselves the one from the other.

"Abram dwelled in the land of Canaan, and Lot dwelled in the cities of the plain, and pitched his tent toward Sodom.

"But the men of Sodom were wicked and sinners before the Lord exceedingly." (Genesis 13:2, 5-13.)

Why Lot went in the direction of Sodom is a question. It must have been his desire for more wealth. He took the land that he felt was most desirable, but it reached one of the most wicked places on earth—Sodom, where the people were "wicked and sinners before the Lord exceedingly." Though Lot must have known this, nevertheless he made his home among them. This is emphasized in the incident preceding the destruction of "the cities of the plains." (Genesis 19:1-11.)

But it was different with Abraham. He was generous and fair with Lot, allowing him first choice in the division of the land.

It is more than interesting that as he left Haran to go to Egypt, he said to the Lord: "I will do well to hearken unto thy voice." (Abraham 2:13.) What a lesson that was! What a lesson for all mankind!

And this is what he did. Each time the Lord told him to move, he hearkened unto his voice. When the Lord told him to save his life by presenting Sarah as his sister, he did so, and his life was spared.

It is remarkable how frequently in his travels Abraham built altars and offered sacrifices to the Lord.

Giving up the land that Lot took must not have been easy for Abraham, for "all the plains of Jordan [which Lot chose] . . . was well watered every where . . . even as the garden of the Lord, like the land of Egypt." (Genesis 13:10.) Indeed, it was a land flowing with milk and honey. But what a contrast later, when famine came and water was no longer available!

Lot went his way, toward wicked Sodom; but the Lord was with Abraham, and once again he renewed his promise to this "father of the faithful."

"And the Lord said unto Abram, after that Lot was separated from him, Lift up now thine eyes, and look from the place where thou art northward, and southward, and eastward, and westward:

"For all the land which thou seest, to thee will I give it, and thy seed for ever.

"And I will make thy seed as the dust of the earth: so that if a man can number the dust of the earth, then shall thy seed also be numbered.

"Arise, walk through the land in the length of it and in the breadth of it; for I will give it unto thee.

"Then Abram removed his tent, and came and dwelt in the

plain of Mamre, which is in Hebron, and built there an altar unto
the Lord.'' (Genesis 13:14-18.)

Chapter 19

HAGAR AND SARAH

The promises made to Abraham that he and Sarah would yet have a vast posterity seemed ironic in the face of her sterility. The Lord had told them that great nations would come of them, but they had to wait some fifty years for the birth of their son, Isaac.

Sarah did not at any time feel certain that the Lord would keep his word. She had laughed when the promise was made, realizing that she was beyond the usual childbearing period.

In her impatience, as she waited for a child of her own, and not too sure that she would ever have one, she began to feel that posterity would have to come in another way. She felt disgraced in not having become a mother. It was customary in those days when a wife was sterile that she might give her husband a servant woman to serve as her proxy in bearing children to be credited to herself. Hagar was such a servant. The scripture reads:

"Now Sarai Abram's wife bare him no children: and she had an handmaid, an Egyptian, whose name was Hagar.

"And Sarai said unto Abram, Behold now, the Lord hath restrained me from bearing: I pray thee, go in unto my maid; it may be that I may obtain children by her. And Abram hearkened to the voice of Sarai.

"And Sarai Abram's wife took Hagar her maid the Egyptian, after Abram had dwelt ten years in the land of Canaan, and gave her to her husband Abram to be his wife." (Genesis 16:1-3.)

But trouble immediately followed. As soon as Hagar became pregnant and realized that she was called upon to produce children to the name of her sterile mistress, herself being merely used for this purpose, she began to hate Sarah deeply.

Sarah immediately repented of what she had done, and said to Abraham: "My wrong be upon thee: I have given my maid into thy bosom; and when she saw that she had conceived, I was despised in her eyes: the Lord judge between me and thee.

"But Abram said unto Sarai, Behold, thy maid is in thy hand; do to her as it pleaseth thee. And when Sarai dealt hardly with her, she fled from her face.

"And the angel of the Lord found her by a fountain of water in the wilderness, by the fountain in the way in Shur.

"And he said, Hagar, Sarai's maid, whence camest thou? and whither wilt thou go? And she said, I flee from the face of my mistress Sarai.

"And the angel of the Lord said unto her, Return to thy mistress, and submit thyself under her hands.

"And the angel of the Lord said unto her, I will multiply thy seed exceedingly, that it shall not be numbered for multitude.

"And the angel of the Lord said unto her, Behold, thou art with child, and shalt bear a son, and shalt call his name Ishmael; because the Lord hath heard thy affliction.

"And he will be a wild man; his hand will be against every man, and every man's hand against him; and he shall dwell in the presence of all his brethren.

"And she called the name of the Lord that spake unto her, Thou God seest me: for she said, Have I also here looked after him that seeth me?

"Wherefore the well was called Beerlahairoi; behold, it is between Kadesh and Bered.

"And Hagar bare Abram a son: and Abram called his son's name, which Hagar bare, Ishmael.

"And Abram was fourscore and six years old, when Hagar bore Ishmael to Abram." (Genesis 16:5-16.)

Slavery was common throughout the Middle East in those days, and for years before and afterward. Human beings were sold as property, just as in the pre-Civil War days in the United States. There was international slave trade between the various countries.

As the scripture indicates, Hagar was an Egyptian. However, how Abraham came to possess her is not mentioned.

Slavery was common in Egypt. The Israelites later were in bondage there. But it was also allowed in the time of Moses among the Lord's own people. Certain of the Mosaic laws prescribed the manner of dealing with such servants. The scripture indicates that it began with Canaan, the son of Ham. It came as a curse from Noah, his grandfather. And indeed slavery is a curse. Not all slaves were descendants of Canaan, however, for war prisoners were usually made slaves if they were not killed.

The curse of Canaan came about in this way:

"And Noah began to be an husbandman, and he planted a vineyard:

"And he drank of the wine, and was drunken; and he was uncovered within his tent.

"And Ham, the father of Canaan, saw the nakedness of his father, and told his two brethren without.

"And Shem and Japheth took a garment, and laid it upon both their shoulders, and went backward, and covered the nakedness of their father; and their faces were backward, and they saw not their father's nakedness.

"And Noah awoke from his wine, and knew what his younger son had done unto him.

"And he said, Cursed be Canaan; a servant of servants shall he be unto his brethren.

"And he said, Blessed be the Lord God of Shem; and Canaan shall be his servant.

"God shall enlarge Japheth, and he shall dwell in the tents of Shem; and Canaan shall be his servant." (Genesis 9:20-27.)

When the law of circumcision was given, it included slaves, as we read in Genesis 17:13: "He that is born in thy house, and he that is bought with thy money, must needs be circumcised: and my covenant shall be in your flesh for an everlasting covenant." Note the words "He that is bought with thy money," showing that the transaction in slavery was a purchase arrangement.

Examples of this in the days of Moses are shown in these passages:

"If thou buy an Hebrew servant, six years he shall serve: and in the seventh he shall go out free for nothing.

"If he came in by himself, he shall go out by himself: if he were married, then his wife shall go out with him.

"If his master have given him a wife, and she have born him sons or daughters; the wife and her children shall be her master's, and he shall go out by himself.

"And if the servant shall plainly say, I love my master, my wife, and my children; I will not go out free:

"Then his master shall bring him unto the judges; he shall also bring him to the door, or unto the door post; and his master shall bore his ear through with an aul; and he shall serve him for ever.

"And if a man sell his daughter to be a maidservant, she shall not go out as the menservants do.

"If she please not her master, who hath betrothed her to himself, then shall he let her be redeemed: to sell her unto a strange nation he shall have no power, seeing he hath dealt deceitfully with her.

"And if he have betrothed her unto his son, he shall deal with her after the manner of daughters.

"If he take him another wife; her food, her raiment, and her duty of marriage, shall he not diminish.

"And if he do not these three unto her, then shall she go out free without money." (Exodus 21:2-11.)

And we have this from Deuteronomy:

"And if thy brother, an Hebrew man, or an Hebrew woman, be sold unto thee, and serve thee six years; then in the seventh year thou shalt let him go free from thee.

"And when thou sendest him out free from thee, thou shalt not let him go away empty:

"Thou shalt furnish him liberally out of thy flock, and out of thy floor, and out of thy winepress: of that wherewith the Lord thy God hath blessed thee thou shalt give unto him.

"And thou shalt remember that thou was a bondman in the land of Egypt, and the Lord thy God redeemed thee: therefore I command thee this thing to day.

"And it shall be, if he say unto thee, I will not go away from thee; because he loveth thee and thine house, because he is well with thee;

"Then thou shalt take an aul, and thrust it through his ear unto the door, and he shall be thy servant for ever. And also unto thy maidservant thou shalt do likewise.

"It shall not seem hard unto thee, when thou sendest him away free from thee; for he hath been worth a double hired servant to thee, in serving thee six years: and the Lord thy God shall bless thee in all that thou doest." (Deuteronomy 15:12-18.)

In Jeremiah we read:

"At the end of seven years let ye go every man his brother an Hebrew, which hath been sold unto thee; and when he hath served thee six years, thou shalt let him go free from thee: but your fathers hearkened not unto me, neither inclined their ear.

"And ye were now turned, and had done right in my sight, in proclaiming liberty every man to his neighbour; and ye had made a covenant before me in the house which is called by my name:

"But ye turned and polluted my name, and caused every man his servant, and every man his handmaid, whom ye had set at liberty at their pleasure, to return, and brought them into subjection, to be unto you for servants and for handmaids.

"Therefore thus saith the Lord; Ye have not hearkened unto me, in proclaiming liberty, every one to his brother, and every man to his neighbour: behold, I proclaim a liberty for you, saith the Lord, to the sword, to the pestilence, and to the famine; and I will make you to be removed into all the kingdoms of the earth." (Jeremiah 34:14-17.)

In the book of Joshua we read how one group of people that had deceived the Israelites were made slaves and forced to become hewers of wood and drawers of water. (Joshua 9:23-27.)

When the Lord gave the law of the Sabbath in the Ten Commandments, he spoke of men servants and maid servants. They were probably people in bondage.

In the New Testament, reference is made to servants. (See Matthew 26:51; Luke 7:8.) Were they bondsmen and bondswomen?

It is well known, of course, that the Romans were slave holders, even in Palestine. And note Paul's advice when he wrote to the Ephesians, saying: "Servants, be obedient to them that are your masters according to the flesh, with fear and trembling, in singleness of your heart, as unto Christ." (Ephesians 6:5.)

When Paul wrote to Titus he gave similar advice: "Exhort servants to be obedient unto their own masters, and to please them well in all things; not answering again." (Titus 2:9.)

He wrote to Timothy: "Let as many servants as are under the yoke count their own masters worthy of all honour, that the name of God and his doctrine be not blasphemed. And they that have believing masters, let them not despise them, because they are brethren; but rather do them service, because they are faithful and beloved, partakers of the benefit. These things teach and exhort.'' (1 Timothy 6:1-2.)

Peter gave the same advice, as may be seen in his first epistle: "Servants, be subject to your masters with all fear; not only to the good and gentle, but also to the froward.'' (1 Peter 2:18.)

And the Colossians were told: "Servants, obey in all things your masters according to the flesh; not with eyeservice, as menpleasers; but in singleness of heart, fearing God.'' (Colossians 3:22.)

From these scriptures it becomes obvious that the early Christians made converts among both free men and slaves. These words of the prophets were simply advice to those who were held in bondage but had joined the church. It was no expression condoning slavery at all; it was merely a recognition that slavery did exist and that some of the slaves had joined the church.

That the Lord ever gave justification to the sale and purchase of human slaves is impossible to believe. Slavery came as a curse from Noah, and it remained a curse. God allowed it through the curse of Canaan, but that does not say that he condoned it. Rather, his whole gospel plan is predicated upon freedom— freedom of choice, or, as we call it, free agency. And this for one great reason: that we may be accountable for our own sins. He made this abundantly clear to the Prophet Joseph Smith when he spoke of the United States Constitution. He said, referring to the afflicted Saints:

"It is my will that they should continue to importune for redress, and redemption, by the hands of those who are placed as rulers and are in authority over you—

"According to the laws and constitution of the people, which I have suffered to be established, and should be maintained for the rights and protection of *all flesh* according to just and holy principles;

"That every man may act in doctrine and principle pertaining to futurity, according to the moral agency which I have given unto him, that every man may be accountable for his own sins in the day of judgment.

"Therefore, *it is not right that any man should be in bondage one to another.*

"And for this purpose have I established the Constitution of this land, by the hands of wise men whom I raised up unto this very purpose, and redeemed the land by the shedding of blood.'' (D&C 101:76-80. Italics added.)

For a time the Lord allowed slavery in America, this land of the free, but he did not condone it any more than he condones a bank robbery, although he gives the robber the free agency to sin. Neither did he condone slave trade anciently. How could any slave be held accountable for his own deeds when he was constantly forced to obey another person? The people in the days of Moses were allowed slaves for a reason that we do not know, but the Lord regulated their treatment.

Why Abraham and Sarah had a bondwoman we do not understand. But the Lord heard the cries of Hagar in distress and sent an angel to help her. The actions of the Lord's ancient peoples merely fit into the customs of that day, just as in these days we fit into customs that are not necessarily approved of the Lord. He allows his people free agency, with the understanding that as we violate the rules of truth and right, we must pay the penalty.

Salvation through the gospel is entirely a matter of exercising free agency. Without such freedom there would be no free-will obedience, and without obedience in righteousness we never could develop the Christlike traits of character that are required before we can enter his presence.

Certainly Hagar's slavery was no comfort to anyone. It was a source of continual discord and conflict to Abraham and his whole family. It is still at the root of some of our worst international problems.

Chapter 20

SIGNS OF THE COVENANT

The Lord deals with his people through covenants to remind them of their obligation to serve him.

As the time approached for the fulfillment of his promise to Sarah, he reiterated what he had previously said. A boy would be born to her. But before the fulfillment, he did two important things.

All through Abraham's early years and up to this point in his life, he had been known as Abram and Sarah as Sarai. Now the Lord changed their names, giving further significance to the fulfillment of the divine promises.

Abram had meant "father of height," according to one authority. Abraham means "father of a multitude." The relationship to the promise is quickly seen.

Sarai meant "a princess." That name was now changed to Sarah, indicating that she would become the queenly mother of multitudes.

As the Lord made these changes he said: "Neither shall thy name any more be called Abram, but thy name shall be Abraham; for a father of many nations have I made thee." (Genesis 17:5.)

When he changed Sarai's name, the Lord said to Abraham, "As for Sarai thy wife, thou shalt not call her name Sarai, but Sarah shall her name be. And I will bless her, and give thee a son also of her: yea, I will bless her, and she shall be a mother of nations; kings of people shall be of her." (Genesis 17:15-16.)

Next, the Lord gave a commandment instituting a physical sign of his covenant, a permanent one that would constantly remind Abraham and all his people of their obligation to serve him and have no other gods in their lives. He said:

"This is my covenant, which ye shall keep, between me and you and thy seed after thee; Every man child among you shall be circumcised.

"And ye shall circumcise the flesh of your foreskin; and it shall be a token of the covenant betwixt me and you.

"And he that is eight days old shall be circumcised among you, every man child in your generations, he that is born in the house, or bought with money of any stranger, which is not of thy seed.

"He that is born in thy house, and he that is bought with thy money, must needs be circumcised: and my covenant shall be in your flesh for an everlasting covenant.

"And the uncircumcised man child whose flesh of his foreskin is not circumcised, that soul shall be cut off from his people; he hath broken my covenant."

Again the Lord announced his promise that Sarah would have a child. But Abraham doubted. He fell on his face "and laughed, and said in his heart, Shall a child be born unto him that is an hundred years old? and shall Sarah, that is ninety, bear?" Sarah too rejoiced at the idea.

Not believing, Abraham then prayed that Ishmael could be favored: "O that Ishmael might live before thee!"

But the Lord repeated his promise and removed all doubt: "Sarah thy wife shall bear thee a son indeed; and thou shalt call his name Isaac: and I will establish my covenant with him for an everlasting covenant, and with his seed after him."

To satisfy Abraham's query about Ishmael, the Lord said: "And as for Ishmael, I have heard thee: Behold, I have blessed him, and will make him fruitful, and will multiply him exceedingly; twelve princes shall he beget, and I will make him a great nation. But my covenant will I establish with Isaac, which Sarah shall bear unto thee at this set time in the next year. And he left off talking with him, and God went up from Abraham." (Genesis 17:20-22.)

There was no more doubt. Abraham accepted the covenant and the sign of the covenant.

"And Abraham took Ishmael his son, and all that were born in his house, and all that were bought with his money, every male among the men of Abraham's house; and circumcised the flesh of their foreskin in the selfsame day, as God had said unto him.

"And Abraham was ninety years old and nine, when he was circumcised in the flesh of his foreskin.

"And Ishmael his son was thirteen years old, when he was circumcised in the flesh of his foreskin.

"In the selfsame day was Abraham circumcised, and Ishmael his son.

"And all the men of his house, born in the house, and bought with money of the stranger, were circumcised with him." (Genesis 17:10-27.)

Inasmuch as the promise of the Lord pertained to posterity, it was appropriate that the reproductive organ be circumcised as a physical and permanent reminder of the covenant. Since everyone was expected to obey the Lord's commandments in order to merit his blessings, every man of that time therefore was required to carry on his person the permanent reminder of the covenant, and that reminder was circumcision.

The expression "the uncircumcised" referred in ancient times to the gentile nations and was often used as a term of reproach. (See Judges 14:3; 1 Samuel 17:26, 36; 2 Samuel 1:20.)

Any foreigners joining the Jewish community were required to be circumcised. (See Genesis 34:14-17.) The expression "the circumcision" as used in the New Testament distinguished between circumcised Jews and uncircumcised gentiles. (See Galations 2:8; Colossians 4:11.) As the apostle Paul used the expression, it had a spiritual significance having to do with putting away the sins of the flesh. (See Colossians 2:11.)

In the modern Church of Jesus Christ, no such requirement is made. We have other covenants and other signs instead. For example, we take upon ourselves the name of Christ and promise to obey him and keep his commandments. The promise of the Lord in return is that we may be freed of our sins and enter his church. What sign represents that?

It is baptism. Our burial in the water is a symbol of the burial of Christ in the tomb. Our coming forth from the waters of baptism is representative of his resurrection from the tomb. It is in baptism that we receive remission of our sins and take upon ourselves his holy name and pledge to serve him.

Another great sign of a covenant that we have today is the sacrament of the Lord's Supper. We partake of the broken bread in remembrance of the Lord's flesh, which was broken on the cross. We drink of the cup in remembrance of his blood, which was shed on the cross. The covenant is detailed in the words of the prayers offered in the administration of the sacrament.

In the days of Paul there was a dispute between gentiles and Jews coming into the Church. Paul argued that the gentiles were not subject to circumcision because it was related to the "old covenant," as were burnt offerings. No Christians are required by the Lord to submit to circumcision. In the atonement of Christ all things became new and old things were "done away." (See Acts 15; 3 Nephi 15.)

As with the early Christians, we of today live under the new law.

Chapter 21

THE THREE VISITORS

Abraham lived in a tent on the plains of Mamre, where the Lord appeared to him and talked with him at length. It was on this occasion that Sarah laughed within herself when the Lord promised them a son in their old age.

"And he [the Lord] said, I will certainly return unto thee according to the time of life; and, lo, Sarah thy wife shall have a son. And Sarah heard it in the tent door, which was behind him.

"Now Abraham and Sarah were old and well stricken in age; and it ceased to be with Sarah after the manner of women.

"Therefore Sarah laughed within herself, saying, After I am waxed old shall I have pleasure, my lord being old also?

"And the Lord said unto Abraham, Wherefore did Sarah laugh, saying, Shall I of a surety bear a child, which am old?

"Is any thing too hard for the Lord? At the time appointed I will return unto thee, according to the time of life, and Sarah shall have a son.

"Then Sarah denied, saying, I laughed not; for she was afraid. And he said, Nay; but thou didst laugh." (Genesis 18:10-15.)

On this visit it was made known to Abraham that the Lord planned to destroy the nearby cities of Sodom and Gomorrah. "Their sin is very grievous," he explained.

At the same time other visitors came, angels who were on their way to Sodom prior to its destruction.

Abraham was worried that the Lord would destroy those cities, wicked as they were, because Lot and his family lived there.

It is not known why Lot would dwell in such a wicked place. He had chosen what he regarded as the best part of Palestine when Abraham gave him a choice, but the land bordered on Sodom. And now he lived there with his many cattle and other possessions. Like many a rancher, it appears he lived in the city while his ranch was out in the open spaces.

When the angels left, the Lord continued visiting with Abraham. "And Abraham drew near, and said, Wilt thou also destroy the righteous with the wicked?

"Peradventure there be fifty righteous within the city: wilt thou also destroy and not spare the place for fifty righteous that are therein?

"That be far from thee to do after this manner, to slay the righteous with the wicked: and that the righteous should be as the wicked, that be far from thee: Shall not the Judge of all the earth do right?

"And the Lord said, If I find fifty righteous within the city, then I will spare all the place for their sakes.

"And Abraham answered and said, Behold now, I have taken upon me to speak unto the Lord, which am but dust and ashes:

"Peradventure there shall lack five of the fifty righteous: wilt thou destroy all the city for lack of five? And he said, If I find there forty and five, I will not destroy it.

"And he spake unto him yet again, and said, Peradventure there shall be forty found there. And he said, I will not do it for forty's sake.

"And he said unto him, Oh let not the Lord be angry, and I will speak: Peradventure there shall thirty be found there. And he said, I will not do it, if I find thirty there.

"And he said, Behold now, I have taken upon me to speak unto the Lord: Peradventure there shall be twenty found there. And he said, I will not destroy it for twenty's sake.

"And he said, Oh let not the Lord be angry, and I will speak yet but this once: Peradventure ten shall be found there. And he said, I will not destroy it for ten's sake." (Genesis 18:23-32.)

But the angels went on to the plain. When they arrived, Lot was sitting "in the gate of Sodom: and Lot seeing them rose up to meet them; and he bowed himself with his face toward the ground;

"And he said, Behold now, my lords, turn in, I pray you, into your servant's house, and tarry all night, and wash your feet, and ye shall rise up early, and go on your ways. And they said, Nay; but we will abide in the street all night.

''And he pressed upon them greatly; and they turned in unto him, and entered into his house; and he made them a feast, and did bake unleavened bread, and they did eat.'' (Genesis 19:1-3.)

The men of the city were guilty of sex perversions, and when they saw the two angels enter Lot's house, they lusted after them. Because of the city's dreadful iniquity, there has come down to us the word *sodomy*, which is related to one of Sodom's kinds of sin.

When Lot kept the angels in the house, the men outside the door threatened him. He went out to entreat with them, but when the uproar at the door increased, the angels pulled Lot back inside. They then ''smote the men that were at the door of the house with blindness, both small and great.''

The angels said to Lot: ''Hast thou here any besides? son in law, and thy sons, and thy daughters, and whatsoever thou hast in the city, bring them out of this place:

''For we will destroy this place, because the cry of them is waxen great before the face of the Lord; and the Lord hath sent us to destroy it.

''And Lot went out, and spake unto his sons in law, which married his daughters, and said, Up, get you out of this place; for the Lord will destroy this city. But he seemed as one that mocked unto his sons in law.

''And when the morning arose, then the angels hastened Lot, saying, Arise, take thy wife, and thy two daughters, which are here; lest thou be consumed in the iniquity of the city.

''And while he lingered, the men laid hold upon his hand, and upon the hand of his wife, and upon the hand of his two daughters; the Lord being merciful unto him: and they brought him forth, and set him without the city.

''And it came to pass, when they had brought them forth abroad, that he said, Escape for thy life; look not behind thee, neither stay thou in all the plain; escape to the mountain, lest thou be consumed.

''And Lot said unto them, Oh, not so, my Lord:

''Behold now, thy servant hath found grace in thy sight, and thou hast magnified thy mercy, which thou hast shewed unto me in saving my life; and I cannot escape to the mountain, lest some evil take me, and I die:

''Behold now, this city is near to flee unto, and it is a little

one: Oh, let me escape thither, (is it not a little one?) and my soul
shall live.

"And he said unto him, See, I have accepted thee concerning
this thing also, that I will not overthrow this city, for the which
thou hast spoken.

"Haste thee, escape thither; for I cannot do any thing till thou
be come thither. Therefore the name of the city was called Zoar.

"The sun was risen upon the earth when Lot entered into
Zoar.

"Then the Lord rained upon Sodom and upon Gomorrah
brimstone and fire from the Lord out of heaven;

"And he overthrew those cities, and all the plain, and all the
inhabitants of the cities, and that which grew upon the ground.

"But his wife looked back from behind him, and she became
a pillar of salt.

"And Abraham gat up early in the morning to the place
where he stood before the Lord:

"And he looked toward Sodom and Gomorrah, and toward
all the land of the plain, and beheld, and, lo, the smoke of the
country went up as the smoke of a furnace.

"And it came to pass, when God destroyed the cities of the
plain, that God remembered Abraham, and sent Lot out of the
midst of the overthrow, when he overthrew the cities in the which
Lot dwelt." (Genesis 19:12-29.)

So the cities were destroyed, and Lot was saved for Abraham's sake.

Chapter 22

ABRAHAM AND MELCHIZEDEK

The people of Canaan were not united into one nation. Each city had its own separate government, its own king, and its own army. They were what the Greeks called city-states, and in this regard they resembled ancient Athens and Sparta.

The Canaanite cities were usually small, some of them occupying only a few acres of ground. Jericho is reported by archaeologists to have contained no more than about six to ten acres.

The kingdoms warred against each other from time to time, a condition that continued even until the days of Moses, a half millennium later. While Lot was living in Sodom, and before its destruction, that city was attacked and its inhabitants were taken away as prisoners. In this battle Lot and his family were seized and carried away with other prisoners. The record reads:

"And there went out the king of Sodom, and the king of Gomorrah, and the king of Admah, and the king of Zeboiim, and the king of Bela (the same is Zoar;) and they joined battle with them in the vale of Siddim;

"With Chedorlaomer the king of Elam, and with Tidal king of nations, and Amraphel king of Shinar, and Arioch king of Ellasar; four kings with five.

"And the vale of Siddim was full of slimepits; and the kings of Sodom and Gomorrah fled, and fell there; and they that remained fled to the mountain.

"And they took all the goods of Sodom and Gomorrah, and all their victuals, and went their way.

"And they took Lot, Abram's brother's son, who dwelt in Sodom, and his goods, and departed.

"And there came one that had escaped, and told Abram the Hebrew; for he dwelt in the plain of Mamre the Amorite, brother of Eshcol, and brother of Aner: and these were confederate with Abram.

"And when Abram heard that his brother was taken captive, he armed his trained servants, born in his own house, three hundred and eighteen, and pursued them unto Dan.

"And he divided himself against them, he and his servants, by night, and smote them, and pursued them unto Hobah, which is on the left hand of Damascus.

"And he brought back all the goods, and also brought again his brother Lot, and his goods, and the women also, and the people.

"And the king of Sodom went out to meet him after his return from the slaughter of Chedorlaomer, and of the kings that were with him, at the valley of Shaveh, which is the king's dale.

"And Melchizedek king of Salem brought forth bread and wine: and he was the priest of the most high God.

"And he blessed him, and said, Blessed be Abram of the most high God, possessor of heaven and earth:

"And blessed be the most high God, which hath delivered thine enemies into thy hand. And he gave him tithes of all.

"And the king of Sodom said unto Abram, Give me the persons, and take the goods to thyself.

"And Abram said to the king of Sodom, I have lift up mine hand unto the Lord, the most high God, the possessor of heaven and earth,

"That I will not take from a thread even to a shoelatchet, and that I will not take any thing that is thine, lest thou shouldest say, I have made Abram rich:

"Save only that which the young men have eaten, and the portion of the men which went with me, Aner, Eshcol, and Mamre; let them take their portion." (Genesis 14:8-24.)

The Prophet Joseph Smith wrote this concerning the association of Melchizedek and Abraham:

"Now Melchizedek was a man of faith, who wrought righteousness; and when a child he feared God, and stopped the mouths of lions, and quenched the violence of fire.

"And thus, having been approved of God, he was ordained an high priest after the order of the covenant which God made with Enoch,

"It being after the order of the Son of God; which order came, not by man, nor the will of man; neither by father nor mother; neither by beginning of days nor end of years; but of God;

"And it was delivered unto men by the calling of his own voice, according to his own will, unto as many as believed on his name.

"For God having sworn unto Enoch and unto his seed with an oath by himself; that every one being ordained after this order and calling should have power, by faith, to break mountains, to divide the seas, to dry up waters, to turn them out of their course;

"To put at defiance the armies of nations, to divide the earth, to break every band, to stand in the presence of God; to do all things according to his will, according to his command, subdue principalities and powers; and this by the will of the Son of God which was from before the foundation of the world.

"And men having this faith, coming up unto this order of God, were translated and taken up into heaven.

"And now, Melchizedek was a priest of this order; therefore he obtained peace in Salem, and was called the Prince of peace.

"And his people wrought righteousness, and obtained heaven, and sought for the city of Enoch which God had before taken, separating it from the earth, having reserved it unto the latter days, or the end of the world;

"And hath said, and sworn with an oath, that the heavens and the earth should come together; and the sons of God should be tried so as by fire.

"And this Melchizedek, having thus established righteousness, was called the king of heaven by his people, or, in other words, the King of peace.

"And he lifted up his voice, and he blessed Abram, being the high priest, and the keeper of the storehouse of God;

"Him whom God had appointed to receive tithes for the poor. Wherefore, Abram paid unto him tithes of all that he had, of all the riches which he possessed, which God had given him more than that which he had need.

"And it came to pass, that God blessed Abram, and gave unto him riches, and honor, and lands for an everlasting possession; according to the covenant which he had made, and according to the blessing wherewith Melchizedek had blessed him." (JST Genesis 14:26-40.)

This from the Prophet brings out things never before known about Melchizedek. Among them are these:

1. When Melchizedek was but a child, he stopped the mouths of lions and quenched the violence of fire.

2. His order of the priesthood was after the order of Enoch, which was after the Order of the Son of God. Hence Melchizedek was after the order of those men who were translated and taken into heaven. And so are Melchizedek Priesthood holders who live in this modern dispensation, for it is the same priesthood.

3. He was the keeper of the storehouse of God, and as such he received the tithes of Abraham.

When the Book of Mormon discusses Melchizedek, it records:

"Now this Melchizedek was a king over the land of Salem; and his people had waxed strong in iniquity and abomination; yea, they had all gone astray; they were full of all manner of wickedness;

"But Melchizedek having exercised mighty faith, and received the office of the high priesthood according to the holy order of God, did preach repentance unto his people. And behold, they did repent; and Melchizedek did establish peace in the land in his days; therefore he was called the prince of peace, for he was the king of Salem; and he did reign under his father.

"Now, there were many before him, and also there were many afterwards, but none were greater; therefore, of him they have more particularly made mention." (Alma 13:17-19.)

The line of the priesthood held by Melchizedek is traced in the Doctrine and Covenants as follows:

"And Esaias received it under the hand of God.

"Esaias also lived in the days of Abraham, and was blessed of him—

"Which Abraham received the priesthood from Melchizedek, who received it through the lineage of his fathers, even till Noah;

"And from Noah till Enoch, through the lineage of their fathers;

"And from Enoch to Abel, who was slain by the conspiracy of his brother, who received the priesthood by the commandment of God, by the hand of his father Adam, who was the first man—

"Which priesthood continueth in the church of God in all generations, and is without beginning of days or end of years." (D&C 84:12-17.)

Chapter 23

MELCHIZEDEK AND JOSEPH SMITH

As seen in the previous chapter, the Prophet Joseph Smith has given us more information concerning Melchizedek than we have obtained from any other source. But more than just information has been given. The authority of the priesthood that was called after Melchizedek was conferred on Joseph Smith.

Without priesthood, The Church of Jesus Christ of Latter-day Saints could not have been organized; it would never have been restored; it could not function. As the Doctrine and Covenants explains, the Holy Priesthood "continueth in the church of God in all generations, and is without beginning of days or end of years."

The priesthood of Aaron "continueth and abideth forever with the priesthood which is after the holiest order of God.

"And this greater priesthood administereth the gospel and holdeth the key of the mysteries of the kingdom, even the key of the knowledge of God.

"Therefore, in the ordinances thereof, the power of godliness is manifest.

"And without the ordinances thereof, and the authority of the priesthood, the power of godliness is not manifest unto men in the flesh;

"For without this no man can see the face of God, even the Father, and live." (D&C 84:17-22.)

It will be remembered that when the Prophet Joseph went into the woods to pray the Lord told him that the existing churches had a form of godliness, but they denied the power thereof. (Joseph Smith—History 1:19.) Section 84 of the Doctrine and Covenants introduces further light on this point. Note that it says that where the ordinances are not, and where the true authority is not, the power of godliness is not manifest. The various churches lacked the true ordinances and they lacked the true authority and hence had none of the power of godliness. They could not manifest something that they did not have. It becomes evident then that this power had to be restored in these last days. Without it the Church could not exist.

With this Holy Priesthood came great promises, too, for the Lord said:

"And also all they who receive this priesthood receive me, saith the Lord;

"For he that receiveth my servants receiveth me;

"And he that receiveth me receiveth my Father;

"And he that receiveth my Father receiveth my Father's kingdom; therefore all that my Father hath shall be given unto him.

"And this is according to the oath and covenant which belongeth to the priesthood.

"Therefore, all those who receive the priesthood, receive this oath and covenant of my Father, which he cannot break, neither can it be moved.

"But whoso breaketh this covenant after he hath received it, and altogether turneth therefrom, shall not have forgiveness of sins in this world nor in the world to come.

"And wo unto all those who come not unto this priesthood which ye have received, which I now confirm upon you who are present this day, by mine own voice out of the heavens; and even I have given the heavenly hosts and mine angels charge concerning you." (D&C 84:35-42.)

This was the Lord's part of the covenant of the priesthood. Our part is as follows: "For you shall live by every word that proceedeth forth from the mouth of God." (D&C 84:44.)

To illustrate the need for a continuity of this priesthood in the Church, together with its covenant, the Lord further said:

"And every one that hearkeneth to the voice of the Spirit cometh unto God, even the Father.

"And the Father teacheth him of the covenant which he has renewed and confirmed upon you, which is confirmed upon you for your sakes, and not for your sakes only, but for the sake of the whole world.

"And the whole world lieth in sin, and groaneth under darkness and under the bondage of sin.

"And by this you may know they are under the bondage of sin, because they come not unto me.

"For whoso cometh not unto me is under the bondage of sin.

"And whoso receiveth not my voice is not acquainted with my voice, and is not of me.

"And by this you may know the righteous from the wicked, and that the whole world groaneth under sin and darkness even now." (D&C 84:47-53.)

The Lord also said of this priesthood:

"There are, in the church, two priesthoods, namely, the Melchizedek and Aaronic, including the Levitical Priesthood.

"Why the first is called the Melchizedek Priesthood is because Melchizedek was such a great high priest.

"Before his day it was called the Holy Priesthood, after the Order of the Son of God.

"But out of respect or reverence to the name of the Supreme Being, to avoid the too frequent repetition of his name, they, the church, in ancient days, called that priesthood after Melchizedek, or the Melchizedek Priesthood.

"All other authorities or offices in the church are appendages to this priesthood.

"But there are two divisions or grand heads—one is the Melchizedek Priesthood, and the other is the Aaronic or Levitical Priesthood.

"The office of an elder comes under the priesthood of Melchizedek.

"The Melchizedek Priesthood holds the right of presidency, and has power and authority over all the offices in the church in all ages of the world, to administer in spiritual things.

"The Presidency of the High Priesthood, after the order of Melchizedek, have a right to officiate in all the offices in the church.

"High priests after the order of the Melchizedek Priesthood have a right to officiate in their own standing, under the direction of the presidency, in administering spiritual things, and also in the office of an elder, priest (of the Levitical order), teacher, deacon, and member." (D&C 107:1-10.)

The offices of the First Presidency and the Council of the Twelve arise out of this priesthood, and, indeed, the other offices of the Church do also. (See D&C 107.)

All the powers of these priesthoods were conferred upon the Prophet Joseph Smith by the visitation of holy angels. John the Baptist began the series when he conferred upon Joseph and Oliver the Aaronic Priesthood on May 15, 1829. This was followed shortly by the visitation of Peter, James, and John, who conferred upon these same two men the Holy Melchizedek Priesthood, together with the apostleship.

Many powers and keys within this priesthood were conferred by other angels. Elijah came, bestowing the keys of his office to turn the hearts of fathers and children to each other in order that the great temple program of the Church could proceed with power. (Malachi 4:5-6.) Moses came with the authority to gather Israel from the four quarters of the earth and the ten tribes from the land of the north. (D&C 110.) Elias came with the keys of the dispensation of Abraham. This was the dispensation to which Melchizedek belonged since he was contemporary with Abraham, and was "keeper of the Lord's storehouse."

The Prophet wrote the following, describing heavenly visitations in this dispensation:

"Now, what do we hear in the gospel which we have received? A voice of gladness! A voice of mercy from heaven; and a voice of truth out of the earth; glad tidings for the dead; a voice of gladness for the living and the dead; glad tidings of great joy. How beautiful upon the mountains are the feet of those that bring glad tidings of good things, and that say unto Zion: Behold, thy God reigneth! As the dews of Carmel, so shall the knowledge of God descend upon them!

"And again, what do we hear? Glad tidings from Cumorah! Moroni, an angel from heaven, declaring the fulfillment of the prophets—the book to be revealed. A voice of the Lord in the wilderness of Fayette, Seneca county, declaring the three witnesses to bear record of the book! The voice of Michael on the banks of the Susquehanna, detecting the devil when he appeared as an angel of light! The voice of Peter, James, and John in the wilderness between Harmony, Susquehanna county, and Colesville, Broome county, on the Susquehanna river, declaring themselves as possessing the keys of the kingdom, and of the dispensation of the fulness of times!

"And again, the voice of God in the chamber of old Father Whitmer, in Fayette, Seneca county, and at sundry times, and in divers places through all the travels and tribulations of this Church of Jesus Christ of Latter-day Saints! And the voice of Michael, the archangel; the voice of Gabriel, and of Raphael, and of divers angels, from Michael or Adam down to the present time, all declaring their dispensation, their rights, their keys, their honors, their majesty and glory, and the power of their priesthood; giving line upon line, precept upon precept; here a little, and there a little; giving us consolation by holding forth that which is to come, confirming our hope!'' (D&C 128:19-21.)

This is the manner in which the powers of all other dispensations were brought together in this, the Dispensation of the Fulness of Times. That is what makes this the fulness of times.

So now Peter's prediction in Acts 3:21 was fulfilled. All the great prophets ''since the world began'' came to Joseph Smith, that noble servant of God who was chosen as the instrument through whom all would be restored. Each gave his powers, his keys, and his authorities to Joseph. And why? To prepare for the second coming of Christ, thus equipping the Church to build the kingdom to which the Lord will come.

But Joseph was martyred. What became of all those powers when he died? Did he take them with him into the grave? And if he did, how could—how can—the Church carry on the work? Authority in the ministry is required to make all things valid. What became of all those keys which the angels gave to Joseph Smith?

Joseph knew beforehand that he was to become a martyr. He was impressed with this fact for some time prior to his death. He knew that he himself was but the instrument through whom the restoration came. He fully realized that the keys given to him must continue in the Church or it could not function. Therefore, he conferred all these powers upon the Twelve Apostles who were chosen of God to carry on after his death.

Chapter 24

THE KEYS TRANSMITTED

Prior to his death the Prophet Joseph Smith conferred upon the Twelve Apostles of the Church all the keys and power that the angels had bestowed upon him as part of the restoration of the gospel.

This empowered the Twelve to become the presiding body after his death, so that they could direct the work of the Church and continue to carry on its great mission without interruption.

On February 27, 1835, according to minutes kept by Oliver Cowdery, in answer to a question pertaining to the importance of the calling of the Twelve and how their calling was different from other callings in the Church, the Prophet said: "They are to hold the keys of this ministry, to unlock the door of the Kingdom of heaven unto all nations, and to preach the Gospel to every creature." (HC 2:200.) Who but Joseph Smith could perform such an ordination?

In connection with the dedicatory services in the Kirtland Temple, the Prophet on March 27, 1836, wrote this in his own history: "I then called upon the quorums and congregation of saints to acknowledge the Twelve Apostles, who were present, as Prophets, Seers, Revelators, and special witnesses to all the nations of the earth, holding the keys of the kingdom, to unlock it, or cause it to be done, among them, and uphold them by their prayers, which they assented to by rising." (HC 2:417.)

On August 16, 1841, the Prophet addressed a conference of the Saints. The official history of the Church, approved by the Prophet and included in his own writings, says of this address:

"President Joseph Smith now arriving, proceeded to state to the conference at considerable length, the object of their present meeting, and, in addition to what President Young had stated in the morning, said that the time had come when the Twelve should be called upon to stand in their place next to the First Presidency, and attend to the settling of emigrants and the business of the Church at the stakes, and assist to bear off the kingdom victoriously to the nations. . . . Moved, seconded and carried, that the conference approve of the instructions of President Smith in relation to the Twelve, and that they proceed accordingly to attend to the duties of their office.'' (HC 4:403.)

Heber C. Kimball said in an address in Salt Lake City October 8, 1852: ''As to the power and authority vested in brother Brigham, do I doubt it? Have I the least hesitation as to his calling as the President of this Church? No, no more than I have that God sits upon His throne. He has the same authority that brother Joseph had. That authority was in the Twelve, and since brother Joseph stepped behind the vail, brother Brigham is his lawful successor. I bear testimony of what brother Joseph said on the stand at Nauvoo, and I presume hundreds here can bear witness of the same. Said he, 'These men that are set here behind me on this stand, I have conferred upon them all the power, Priesthood, and authority that God ever conferred upon me.' '' (*Journal of Discourses* 1:206.)

Wilford Woodruff, in general conference in April 1898, said: ''The last speech that Joseph Smith ever made to the quorum of the Apostles was in a building in Nauvoo, and it was such a speech as I never heard from mortal man before or since. He was clothed upon with the Spirit and power of God. His face was clear as amber. The room was filled as with consuming fire. He stood three hours upon his feet. Said he: 'You Apostles of the Lamb of God have been chosen to carry out the purposes of the Lord on the earth. Now, I have received, as the Prophet, seer and revelator, standing at the head of this dispensation, every key, every ordinance, every principle and every Priesthood that belongs to the last dispensation and fulness of times. And I have sealed all these things upon your heads.' '' (*Conference Report*, April 1898, p. 89.)

Brigham Young, in a letter written to Orson Spencer on January 23, 1848, said: ''Joseph told the Twelve, the year before he died, 'there is not one key or power to be bestowed on this church to lead the people into the celestial gate but I have given you, showed you, and talked it over to you; the kingdom is set up, and you have the perfect pattern, and you can go and build up the kingdom, and go in at the celestial gate, taking your train with you.' '' (*Millennial Star* 10:115.)

Heber C. Kimball wrote in the *Times and Seasons*, October 1, 1844: ''Bro. Joseph has passed behind the vail and he pulled off his shoes, and someone else puts them on, until he passes the vail to Bro. Joseph. President Young is our president, and our head, and he puts the shoes on first. . . . The Twelve have received the keys of the kingdom and as long as there is one of them left, he will hold them in preference to any one else.''

Orson Hyde also wrote in *Times and Seasons* September 5, 1844: ''The shafts of the enemy are always aimed at the head first.—Brother Joseph said some time before he was murdered. 'If I am taken away, upon you, the Twelve, will rest the responsibility of leading this people, and do not be bluffed off by any man. . . .

'' 'Now if they kill me you have got all the keys, and all the ordinances and you can confer them upon others, and the hosts of Satan will not be able to tear down the kingdom, as fast as you will be able to build it up; and now says he on your shoulders will the responsibility of leading this people to rest, for the Lord is going to let me rest a while.' ''

From a speech by Orson Hyde, found in the *Journal of Discourses* (13:180), we read: ''I will give you my testimony. In one particular place, in the presence of about sixty men, he [the Prophet Joseph] said, 'My work is about done; I am going to step aside awhile. I am going to rest from my labors; for I have borne the burthen and heat of the day, and now I am going to step aside and rest a little. And I roll the burthen off my shoulders on the shoulders of the Twelve Apostles. Now; said he, round up your shoulders and bear off this kingdom.' ''

Brigham Young writes in the *History of the Church* (7:230):

''I know there are those in our midst who will seek the lives of the Twelve as they did the lives of Joseph and Hyrum. We shall ordain others and give the fulness of the priesthood, so that if we are killed the fulness of the priesthood may remain.

''Joseph conferred upon our heads all the keys and powers belonging to the Apostleship which he himself held before he was taken away, and no man or set of men can get between Joseph and the Twelve in this world or in the world to come.

"How often has Joseph said to the Twelve, 'I have laid the foundation and you must build thereon, for upon your shoulders the kingdom rests.' "

The right to exercise the sealing powers as restored through Elijah the prophet is reserved for the President of the Church himself, and to those to whom he personally delegates that privilege. With reference to this, Parley P. Pratt said in the *Millennial Star*, January 1, 1845: "He proceeded to confer on Elder Young, the president of the Twelve, the keys of the sealing power as conferred in the last days by the spirit and power of Elijah, in order to seal the hearts of the fathers to the children and the hearts of the children to the fathers, lest the whole earth should be smitten with a curse." (HC 5:151.)

On Monday, July 2, 1839, the Prophet Joseph Smith met with the Twelve and other officers of the Church and gave them instructions. He placed a synopsis of his own remarks in his journal, from which the following is taken:

"O ye Twelve! and all Saints! profit by this important *Key*—that in all your trials, troubles, temptations, afflictions, bonds, imprisonments and death, see to it, that you do not betray heaven; that you do not betray Jesus Christ; that you do not betray the brethren; that you do not betray the revelations of God, whether in the Bible, Book of Mormon, or Doctrine and Covenants, or any other that ever was or ever will be given and revealed unto man in this world or that which is to come. Yea, in all your kicking and flounderings, see to it that you do not this thing, lest innocent blood be found upon your skirts, and you go down to hell. All other sins are not to be compared to sinning against the Holy Ghost, and proving a traitor to the brethren.

"I will give you one of the *Keys* of the mysteries of the Kingdom. It is an eternal principle, that has existed with God from all eternity: That man who rises up to condemn others, finding fault with the Church, saying that they are out of the way, while he himself is righteous, then know assuredly, that that man is in the high road to apostasy; and if he does not repent, will apostatize, as God lives. The principle is as correct as the one that Jesus put forth in saying that he who seeketh a sign is an adulterous person; and that principle is eternal, undeviating, and firm as the pillars of heaven." (HC 3:385.)

The Lord said this regarding the exclusive right of the President of the Church to receive revelation for the Church:

"But, behold, verily, verily, I say unto thee, no one shall be appointed to receive commandments and revelations in this church excepting my servant Joseph Smith, Jun., for he receiveth them even as Moses."

"For I have given him the keys of the mysteries, and the revelations which are sealed, until I shall appoint unto them another in his stead." (D&C 28:2, 7.)

"For behold, verily, verily, I say unto you, that ye have received a commandment for a law unto my church, through him whom I have appointed unto you to receive commandments and revelations from my hand.

"And this ye shall know assuredly—that there is none other appointed unto you to receive commandments and revelations until he be taken, if he abide in me.

"But verily, verily, I say unto you, that none else shall be appointed unto this gift except it be through him; for if it be taken from him he shall not have power except to appoint another in his stead. And this shall be a law unto you, that ye receive not the teachings of any that shall come before you as revelations or commandments;

"And this I give unto you that you may not be deceived, that you may know they are not of me.

"For verily I say unto you, that he that is ordained of me shall come in at the gate and be ordained as I have told you before, to teach those revelations which you have received and shall receive through him whom I have appointed." (D&C 43:2-7.)

So the powers of Melchizedek and his contemporaries (of whom Abraham was one), and all the other prophets "since the world began," remained in the Church of Jesus Christ. (Acts 3:21.) By those powers the Church functions now just as in the days of old.

It is significant that there was a storehouse system in Melchizedek's day and that we have such a system in the Church today. Such a storehouse was in the church in the days of Malachi also. He speaks of it as he says: "Bring ye all the tithes into the storehouse, that there may be meat in mine house." (Malachi 3:10.)

Evidently the storehouse keepers received the tithing then, as was the case with Melchizedek. Our storehouses are no different. They are "bishop's storehouses" in the welfare program, operated by the bishops of the wards, who are the men appointed to receive tithes in our day.

Melchizedek was a storekeeper then; our bishops, holding his order of the priesthood, are storekeepers today. Again we see how basic principles in the Church are preserved throughout the ages.

Chapter 25

ISAAC
THE HEIR

The ways of God are not the ways of man, and to some they seem to be foolishness when weighed by worldly wisdom.

The apostle Paul wrote to the Corinthians: ''We preach Christ crucified, unto the Jews a stumblingblock, and unto the Greeks foolishness.'' He said further: ''The foolishness of God is wiser than men; and the weakness of God is stronger than men.''

And then came this significant thing: ''Ye see your calling, brethren, how that not many wise men after the flesh, not many mighty, not many noble, are called: But God hath chosen the foolish things of the world to confound the wise; and God hath chosen the weak things of the world to confound the things which are mighty.'' (1 Corinthians 1:23-27.)

The worldly wise reject the choice of Isaac over Ishmael as being part of the so-called mythology of the Bible. They do the same with the story of Jacob and Esau. And when it comes to the account of Isaac being placed upon the sacrificial altar by his father, they denounce it as a fantastic fairy tale.

But that is worldly ''wisdom.'' God knows what he is about. He sees the end from the beginning, and it was he who separated the descendants of Isaac from those of Ishmael, and those of Jacob from those of Esau.

Why do we now have the various nations if the peoples of the earth were not intentionally separated? Racial differences are seen from one end of the earth to the other with these distinct peoples living pretty much to themselves. The races for the most part are native to lands where they have lived throughout the ages. They did not originate themselves. They were born into their native situations as God planned it.

Paul had this in mind when he told the Greeks on Mars' hill that God ''hath made of one blood [Adam's] all nations of men for to dwell on all the face of the earth, and hath determined the

times before appointed, and the bounds of their habitation.''
(Acts 17:26.)

There is much meaning in that scripture. First, God made all
mankind of one blood—human. That is why various nations can
interbreed—because they are all human. But humans can not interbreed with any other form of life. Human blood is distinct and
is strictly one blood in this sense.

The Lord distributed the various peoples over the face of the
earth into what became nations. He determined their times
(meaning the periods in which they would live). In advance, or,
to use the scriptural word, ''before'' their development, he determined the boundaries of their habitations.

To be fair with us all, the Lord must have based his decisions
on his acquaintance with us in our premortal life. Something
there persuaded him in his wise planning to distribute us and form
us into various nations on earth. This was not left to chance.

Why did he make a difference between Isaac and Ishmael and
between Jacob and Esau? Because he knew of their premortal experience, which we do not. By his foreknowledge, he knew
where they would best be suited for this mortal life, and he placed
them there.

In choosing bloodlines he named Isaac for one group of
people and Ishmael for another. He chose Jacob for the per-
petuity of Isaac's line, and he allowed Esau to go elsewhere.
Similarly, various others were established in the human
bloodstream.

The Lord covenanted through Isaac and not through Ishmael;
but in fairness to him, Ishmael was promised nations, princes,
and kings, even as was Isaac. God is fair to all men. He is just and
no respecter of persons. To each he gives what is best suited for
him, and he can judge this because he was well acquainted with
us in our pre-earth life.

Worldly people do not believe in a premortal existence, but
Latter-day Saints, by the power of revelation, have the facts; they
know that we lived before we came here, and that God understood us well through his infinite perception, even before we
were born. Note how he spoke to Job:

''Where wast thou when I laid the foundations of the earth?
declare, if thou hast understanding.

"Who hath laid the measures thereof, if thou knowest? or who hath stretched the line upon it?

"Whereupon are the foundations thereof fastened? or who laid the corner stone thereof;

"When the morning stars sang together, and all the sons of God shouted for joy?" (Job 38:4-7.)

And consider the words of Solomon which may be applied to our pre-earth life:

"The Lord possessed me in the beginning of his way, before his works of old.

"I was set up from everlasting, from the beginning, or ever the earth was.

"Where there were no depths, I was brought forth; when there were no fountains abounding with water.

"Before the mountains were settled, before the hills was I brought forth:

"While as yet he had not made the earth, nor the fields, nor the highest part of the dust of the world.

"When he prepared the heavens, I was there: when he set a compass upon the face of the depth:

"When he established the clouds above: when he strengthened the fountains of the deep:

"When he gave to the sea his decree, that the waters should not pass his commandment: when he appointed the foundations of the earth:

"Then I was by him, as one brought up with him: and I was daily his delight, rejoicing always before him." (Proverbs 8:22-30.)

Although the Lord made covenants with Isaac, any child of Ishmael may have as many blessings in the Church or in eternity as any child of Isaac—*if* he will but serve Almighty God and keep his commandments. Also, any child of Isaac, regardless of heritage, may *lose* those blessings if he fails to keep the commandments of the Lord.

Do we remember what the Savior said to the Jews about having a privileged status simply because they were of Abraham's seed? He did *not* give them preference over others. The faithful—whether Jews or non-Jews—will be taken into the kingdom, but only on conditions of compliance with the gospel.

Said the Lord: "I say unto you, That many shall come from the east and west, and shall sit down with Abraham, and Isaac, and Jacob, in the kingdom of heaven. But the children of the kingdom shall be cast out into outer darkness: there shall be weeping and gnashing of teeth." (Matthew 8:11-12.)

And what does that mean? That unfaithful descendants of Abraham will be cast out regardless of their blood line, and that some from the east and west of non-Abrahamic lineage will be taken into the kingdom of heaven to dwell there with Abraham if they will obey.

So the Ishmaelites need not worry. If they will be faithful to the teachings of Christ, they can and will go with Abraham into the kingdom of heaven. This will come to them even while covenanted descendants of Abraham are being cast out because of their disobedience.

Obedience is the thing! God, who is no respecter of persons, offers salvation to all who will accept it on terms of true compliance with the commandments, regardless of race.

There is one commandment for all, and that is to become perfect like God. (Matthew 5:48.) And there is only one formula by which this is to be accomplished; that is, obedience to "one Lord, one faith, one baptism"—which is the gospel of Christ. (Ephesians 4:5.) And in the final analysis, race or descent will give no one any special privilege.

When the Jews boasted of their Abrahamic descent, what did the Lord say? "Bring forth therefore fruits meet for repentance: And think not to say within yourselves, We have Abraham to our father: for I say unto you, that God is able of these stones to raise up children unto Abraham." (Matthew 3:8-9.)

God covenanted with Abraham and Isaac because of their premortal faithfulness. But their children who do not live up to the covenant in this life can lose that advantage, while those not of Abraham may obtain that same advantage for themselves if they will accept and live the gospel.

We are God's children and he loves us all. He desires that each of us may be saved in his presence. But we must qualify for our salvation, regardless of racial origins.

Chapter 26

THE WEDDING FEAST

One of the graphic illustrations given us by the Savior pertaining to the availability of salvation to all nations is that which is provided in the parable of the wedding feast:

"And Jesus answered and spake unto them again by parables, and said,

"The kingdom of heaven is like unto a certain king, which made a marriage for his son,

"And sent forth his servants to call them that were bidden to the wedding: and they would not come.

"Again, he sent forth other servants, saying, Tell them which are bidden, Behold, I have prepared my dinner: my oxen and my fatlings are killed, and all things are ready: come unto the marriage.

"But they made light of it, and went their ways, one to his farm, another to his merchandise:

"And the remnant took his servants, and entreated them spitefully, and slew them.

"But when the king heard thereof, he was wroth: and he sent forth his armies, and destroyed those murderers, and burned up their city.

"Then saith he to his servants, The wedding is ready, but they which were bidden were not worthy.

"Go ye therefore into the highways, and as many as ye shall find, bid to the marriage.

"So those servants went out into the highways, and gathered together all as many as they found, both bad and good: and the wedding was furnished with guests." (Matthew 22:1-10.)

It is clearly illustrated that all who are willing to come to the wedding feast (which means into the Lord's kingdom) may come. In the parable no mention is made of Abrahamic or any other ancestral distinction. They were *people* who came—good and bad—and they were made welcome because they complied with the Lord's invitation. But even for them there was one requirement: they had to have a wedding garment.

"And when the king came in to see the guests, he saw there a man which had not on a wedding garment:

"And he saith unto him, Friend, how camest thou in hither not having a wedding garment? And he was speechless.

"Then said the king to the servants, Bind him hand and foot, and take him away, and cast him into outer darkness; there shall be weeping and gnashing of teeth.

"For many are called, but few are chosen." (Matthew 22:11-14.)

And what is the lesson here? It is that those coming into the kingdom, regardless of ancestry, personally must have cleansed themselves of their worldly filth and taken upon them the responsibility of the name (or the garment) of Christ. That is what qualifies them to enter the kingdom.

Obedience! There is no substitute for it and no excuse for being without it if we hope to enter the kingdom, or, to use the expression in the parable, to sit down to the wedding feast.

Although Isaac was given the covenant and Ishmael was not, by means of the subsequent scattering of the blood of Israel among all nations the promises made to Abraham were extended to every tongue and people. Hence the covenant will take in all believers, regardless of their nationality. And what is the reasoning behind all this? It is simple. The Lord commands us to become perfect like our Father in heaven is perfect. (Matthew 5:48.) God wants us, his children, to become like him. That is his work, his glory, and his great objective.

The apostle Paul speaks of the same principle and says that we must achieve to the status of a perfect man, "unto the measure of the stature of the fulness of Christ." (Ephesians 4:13.) That is our destiny.

But gaining perfection is a matter of development, going from teaching to acceptance to application and finally to realization. It is a growth process. Was there ever a plant that achieved its full growth instantly? Was there an animal that did? Was there ever a child who suddenly and without waiting became a man? It is all a process of growth and development.

It is just as unreasonable to suppose that a child can instantly become a man or that a freshman high school student can suddenly earn a doctor's degree from college as it is to suppose that we finite beings can suddenly become infinite, or that we imperfect humans can suddenly become perfect and divine.

That is why we have the gospel plan. It is our pattern of growth and development, and whosoever follows that pattern obtains the desired result regardless of nationality. It is just as certain as the conclusion of a chemical procedure that follows a definite formula.

But people who become doctors or engineers or great musicians need instruction and direction; they need teachers who already know the way. Otherwise there would be no genuine achievement. It is the same with becoming perfect like our Heavenly Father.

The Lord gave us the Church and its organization, headed by apostles and prophets, as the means by which we may achieve perfection. It was established for "the perfecting of the saints, for the work of the ministry, for the edifying of the body of Christ." (Ephesians 4:12.) Hence we must be active in it.

The Lord said that his work and his glory are to bring to pass the immortality and eternal life of man. (Moses 1:39.) And what does that mean? That we may truly become like him—our eternal Heavenly Father!

To enter his presence and become like him, however, we must follow the formula that will bring that condition about. Perfection can be obtained in only one way—by compliance with the principles of perfection. Class privilege or racial preference cannot possibly do this for us.

Everyone may be saved who will accept and serve the Lord. No one will be saved who refuses to do this. Race and ancestry or the lack of them can never help us without true conversion and obedience.

Chapter 27

THEY GO
THEIR WAYS

And God said, Sarah thy wife shall bear thee a son indeed; and thou shalt call his name Isaac: and I will establish my covenant with him for an everlasting covenant, and with his seed after him.

"And as for Ishmael, I have heard thee: Behold, I have blessed him, and will make him fruitful, and will multiply him exceedingly; twelve princes shall he beget, and I will make him a great nation.

"But my covenant will I establish with Isaac, which Sarah shall bear unto thee at this set time in the next year." (Genesis 17:19-21.)

Here the Lord makes a clear distinction between Isaac and Ishmael. Was he unjust? What was the nature of the covenant, and why did it distinguish between the two boys?

God herein was talking about the priestly line, about the choice of his prophets, his ministers here on earth. Through these chosen men, he would labor to save not only their own souls, but also others not even of the covenant.

The Savior made it abundantly clear that all men of every tongue and nation are welcome in the gospel kingdom. He himself labored only among the Jews, but that did not mean he was excluding other nations from salvation. How do we know? Because after his resurrection he sent his disciples to all nations, kindreds, and peoples, telling them: "Go ye into all the world, and preach the gospel to every creature. He that believeth and is baptized shall be saved; but he that believeth not shall be damned." (Mark 16:15-16.)

Nothing is said here about race, national lines, or covenants. The gospel is for all the world, for all peoples. Everyone—regardless of race—who believes, obeys, and is baptized, will be received. It is noted that more than a mere acceptance of Christ is required, however. Baptism and other works must accompany faith. (James 2:14-26.)

When the Lord spoke of his second coming, he added this explanation: ''This gospel of the kingdom shall be preached in all the world for a witness unto all nations; and then shall the end come.'' (Matthew 24:14.)

The restoration of the gospel was to take place ''in the hour of God's judgment'' by means of an angel flying through the heavens. The sacred word then would be preached to ''every nation, and kindred, and tongue, and people.'' (Revelation 14:6.)

Can anyone say that God is a respecter of persons? Is it not clear that he wishes to treat everyone alike? But why are they not all treated alike? Simply because of the individual opinions, obstinacy, and prejudices of various persons.

What was the problem with Ishmael? We must acknowledge that the original choice of a covenant people related to premortal existence. But Ishmael could have had the blessings of the gospel here on earth had he possessed a different attitude, and had he been teachable and kind instead of hateful. If he had possessed love for the infant Isaac instead of hatred; if he had caressed the child instead of mocking him, would not Abraham, the friend of God, have seen to his salvation?

He loved Ishmael. He prayed to God, ''O that Ishmael might live before thee.'' (Genesis 17:18.) Is there not significance in that remark?

Abraham knew that all faithful people will be received by the Lord. Had he suffered from some previous difficulties with Ishmael's boyish attitude? Hagar had hated Sarah for fourteen years. Would not this motherly antagonism have rubbed off on Ishmael, leading to his mocking Isaac?

Ishmael's own attitude is what took him away from the blessings that might have been his! He could have been baptized into the church in those days, and so could Hagar, if they had acted and felt differently! Ishmael was of the blood of Abraham. He was Abraham's son.

The gospel was on the earth in the days of Abraham. Then would Abraham's own flesh and blood, his own son, have been excluded from the blessings of the church—regardless of the covenant—if the boy had been faithful and believing?

To answer that, let us ask another question: Are we admitting Arabs into the modern church? The answer, of course, is yes. Would the Lord give to a modern descendant of Abraham something he would not willingly have given to an immediate son anciently?

On this point President Brigham Young said:

"Who are Israel? They are those who are of the seed of Abraham, who received the promise through their forefathers; and all the rest of the children of men, who receive the truth, are also Israel. My heart is always drawn out for them, whenever I go to the throne of grace.

"Israel is dispersed among all the nations of the earth; the blood of Ephraim is mixed with the blood of all the earth. Abraham's seed is mingled with the rebellious seed through the whole world of mankind.

"The Elders who have arisen in this Church and Kingdom are actually of Israel.

"Those islanders and the natives of this country are of the House of Israel—of the seed of Abraham, and to them pertains the promise; and every soul of them, sooner or later, will be saved in the Kingdom of God, or be destroyed root and branch.

"Again, if a pure Gentile firmly believes the Gospel of Jesus Christ, and yields obedience to it, in such a case I will give you the words of the Prophet Joseph: 'The effect of the Holy Ghost upon a Gentile, is to purge out the old blood, and make him actually of the seed of Abraham.'

"We are to build up and establish Zion, gather the House of Israel, and redeem the nations of the earth. This people have this work to do, whether we live to see it or not. This is all in our hands." (*Discourses of Brigham Young*, p. 437.)

President Joseph Fielding Smith wrote: "The promise was made that in addition to Abraham's direct descendants, all who should receive the Gospel from that time forth, should also become of Abraham's seed by adoption." (*The Way to Perfection*, p. 88.)

He also added: "No person can receive the Gospel without becoming of the seed of Abraham. If they are not of his blood by descent they become so by adoption." (Ibid., p. 89.)

Look at Ishmael and Hagar now from this perspective. See what they missed! What a toll hatred levies on all its victims!

Abraham was instructed: "As many as receive this Gospel shall be called after thy name, and shall be accounted thy seed."

He was told also that through him "shall all the families of the earth be blessed, even with the blessings of the Gospel, which are the blessings of salvation, even of life eternal." (Abraham 2:10-11.)

Would not "all the families of the earth" include Hagar's family and Ishmael's family when he grew up and married—*if* they would do as others receiving those blessings: accept and obey the truth?

Obedience is the thing!

Hagar's hatred, and Ishmael's reflection of her bitterness, closed the door against them. Only love can open it again, the true love of God.

They would not have been refused baptism into the kingdom in those days any more than now, if they had but obeyed. They both were of Abraham's house, one a wife, one a son. So it was attitude, revealed in their obedience or disobedience, that actually drew the line between Isaac and Ishmael. God had no prejudice against Ishmael. The scripture says that he loved the lad. (Genesis 21:20.) He also had due regard for the boy's mother.

When Hagar was in distress because of Sarah's jealousy, and she fled to the desert, it was the Lord who came to the rescue. "And God heard the voice of the lad; and the angel of God called to Hagar out of heaven, and said unto her, What aileth thee, Hagar? Fear not; for God hath heard the voice of the lad where he is. Arise, lift up the lad, and hold him in thine hand; for I will make him a great nation." (Genesis 21:16-18.)

Inasmuch as God loved the lad and promised that he would become a great nation, with kings and princes in his lineage, can anyone say that the Lord was treating him unjustly, especially in view of the boy's hateful attitude?

God grants all people their free agency, including Ishmael and Hagar. But both mother and son allowed bitterness to fill their souls. That is why they received no more of the divine blessings than they did.

Ishmael left the Abrahamic line and went to live in Paran, which is in the wilderness near Sinai. "And his mother took him a wife out of the land of Egypt." (Genesis 21:21.) So it was near Sinai that Ishmael began to rear his family. And now came a further mixture of Egyptian blood with that of Abraham. His descendants have continued to live in that general area ever since.

Isaac, as is known, remained with Abraham, eventually married within his own family circle, and followed after the God of heaven.

With respect to obedience being the source of our blessings, President Brigham Young at one time commented on the disobedience of ancient Israel and the efforts made by Moses to teach them the gospel and bring them back into the kingdom. He said: "If they had been sanctified and holy, the Children of Israel would not have traveled one year with Moses before they would have received their endowments and the Melchizedek Priesthood." (*Discourses of Brigham Young*, p. 106.)

But in their disobedience they traveled for forty years in the wilderness, until the older rebellious generation had died off.

Obedience is the thing, or as we sing in one of our hymns: "Sacrifice brings forth the blessings of heaven." (*Hymns*, no. 147.) The principle applies to all mankind, regardless of race or color or covenants or heritage. There is no progress in the kingdom without obedience.

Chapter 28

THE SACRIFICE OF ISAAC

Is the account of Isaac's sacrifice true or false?

The *Book of Jewish Knowledge*, published by Nathan Ausubel, author of half a dozen large works having to do with the Jewish people, says the sophisticated Jews of modern times regard that event as an ancient morality play. To orthodox Jews for generations past, however, it has been a dominating influence shaping lives and building spirituality.

It is set forth in the Bible as follows:

"And it came to pass after these things, that God did tempt Abraham, and said unto him, Abraham: and he said, Behold, here I am.

"And he said, Take now thy son, thine only son Isaac, whom thou lovest, and get thee into the land of Moriah; and offer him there for a burnt offering upon one of the mountains which I will tell thee of.

"And Abraham rose up early in the morning, and saddled his ass, and took two of his young men with him, and Isaac his son, and clave the wood for the burnt offering, and rose up, and went unto the place of which God had told him.

"Then on the third day Abraham lifted up his eyes, and saw the place afar off.

"And Abraham said unto his young men, Abide ye here with the ass; and I and the lad will go yonder and worship, and come again to you.

"And Abraham took the wood of the burnt offering, and laid it upon Isaac his son; and he took the fire in his hand, and a knife; and they went both of them together.

"And Isaac spake unto Abraham his father, and said, My father: and he said, Here am I, my son. And he said, Behold the fire and the wood: but where is the lamb for a burnt offering?

"And Abraham said, My son, God will provide himself a

lamb for a burnt offering: so they went both of them together.

"And they came to the place which God had told him of; and Abraham built an altar there, and laid the wood in order, and bound Isaac his son, and laid him on the altar upon the wood.

"And Abraham stretched forth his hand, and took the knife to slay his son.

"And the angel of the Lord called unto him out of heaven, and said, Abraham, Abraham: and he said, Here am I.

"And he said, Lay not thine hand upon the lad, neither do thou any thing unto him: for now I know that thou fearest God, seeing thou hast not withheld thy son, thine only son from me.

"And Abraham lifted up his eyes, and looked, and behold behind him a ram caught in a thicket by his horns: and Abraham went and took the ram, and offered him up for a burnt offering in the stead of his son.

"And Abraham called the name of that place Jehovah-jireh: as it is said to this day, In the mount of the Lord it shall be seen.

"And the angel of the Lord called unto Abraham out of heaven the second time.

"And said, By myself have I sworn, saith the Lord, for because thou hast done this thing, and hast not withheld thy son, thine only son:

"That in blessing I will bless thee, and in multiplying I will multiply thy seed as the stars of the heaven, and as the sand which is upon the sea shore; and thy seed shall possess the gate of his enemies;

"And in thy seed shall all the nations of the earth be blessed; because thou hast obeyed my voice.

"So Abraham returned unto his young men, and they rose up and went together to Beersheba; and Abraham dwelt at Beersheba." (Genesis 22:1-19.)

What is the Latter-day Saint point of view?

First of all, we accept the event as having truly happened. It is confirmed repeatedly in modern scripture, and that is our great assurance.

Second, in its way it seems to have presaged the sacrifice of Christ. The Father gave his own Beloved Son to die on the cross.

And next, it is one of the greatest examples of complete faith we know about, and should be a constant inspiration to us.

When the Book of Mormon prophet Jacob discussed the sacrifice of Isaac, he said that it "is a similitude of God and his Only Begotten Son." (Jacob 4:5.)

In section 132 (v. 36) of the Doctrine and Covenants, we have further confirmation that God commanded Abraham to offer up his son Isaac. That scripture specifically says: "Abraham was commanded to offer his son Isaac; nevertheless, it was written: Thou shalt not kill. Abraham, however, did not refuse, and it was accounted unto him for righteousness."

As to the purpose of this event, the Prophet Joseph Smith said: "The sacrifice required of Abraham in the offering up of Isaac, shows that if a man would attain to the keys of the kingdom of an endless life, he must sacrifice all things." (HC 5:555.)

The late Elder Melvin J. Ballard, of the Council of the Twelve, discussed this theme at one time and said:

"I think as I read the story of Abraham's sacrifice of his son Isaac, that our Father is trying to tell us what it cost him to give his Son as a gift to the world.

"You remember the story of how Abraham's son came after long years of waiting, and was looked upon by his worthy sire, Abraham, as more precious than all his other possessions; yet, in the midst of his rejoicing, Abraham was told to take this only son and offer him as a sacrifice to the Lord.

"He responded. Can you feel what was in the heart of Abraham on that occasion? You love your son just as Abraham did; perhaps not quite so much, because of the peculiar circumstances, but what do you think was in his heart when he started away from Mother Sarah and they bade her good bye?

"What do you think was in his heart when he saw Isaac bidding farewell to his mother to take that three days' journey to the appointed place where the sacrifice was to be made? I imagine it was about all Father Abraham could do to keep from showing his great grief and sorrow at that parting, but he and his son trudged along three days toward the appointed place, Isaac carrying the fagots that were to consume the sacrifice. The two travelers rested, finally, at the mountain side, and the men who had accompanied them were told to remain, while Abraham and his son started up the hill.

"The boy then said to his father: 'Why, father, we have the

fagots, we have the fire to burn the sacrifice, but where is the sacrifice?'

"It must have pierced the heart of Father Abraham to hear the trusting and confiding son say: 'You have forgotten the sacrifice.' Looking at the youth, his son of promise, the poor father could only say: 'The Lord will provide.'

"They ascended the mountain, gathered the stones together, and placed the fagots upon them. Then Isaac was bound, hand and foot, kneeling upon the altar. I presume Abraham, like a true father, must have given his son his farewell kiss, his blessing, his love, and his soul must have been drawn out in that hour of agony toward this son who was to die by the hand of his own father. Every step proceeded until the cold steel was drawn, and the hand raised that was to strike the blow to let out the life's blood. When the angel of the Lord said: 'It is enough.'

"Our Father in heaven went through all that and more, for in his case the hand was not stayed. He loved his Son Jesus Christ, better than Abraham ever loved Isaac, for our Father had with him his Son, our Redeemer, in the eternal worlds, faithful and true for ages, standing in a place of trust and honor, and the Father loved him dearly, and yet he allowed this well-beloved Son to descend from his place of glory and honor, where millions did him homage, down to the earth, a condescension that is not within the power of man to conceive of.

"He came to receive the insult, the abuse, and the crown of thorns. God heard the cry of his Son in that moment of great grief and agony, in the garden when, it is said, the pores of his body opened and drops of blood stood upon him and he cried out: 'Father, if thou be willing, remove this cup from me.'

"I ask you, what father and mother could stand by and listen to the cry of their children in distress, in this world, and not render aid and assistance? I have heard of mothers throwing themselves into raging streams when they could not swim a stroke to save their drowning child, rushing into burning buildings, to rescue those whom they loved.

"We can not stand by and listen to those cries without it touches our hearts. The Lord has not given us the power to save our own. He has given us faith and we submit to the inevitable, but he had the power to save, and he loved his Son and he could have saved him.

''He might have rescued him from the insult of the crowds. He might have rescued him when the crown of thorns was placed upon his head. He might have rescued him when the Son, hanging between the two thieves was mocked with, 'Save thyself, and come down from the cross. . . . He saved others; himself he cannot save.'

''He listened to all this. He saw that Son condemned, he saw him drag the cross through the streets of Jerusalem and faint under its load. He saw that Son finally upon Calvary, he saw his body stretched out upon the wooden cross, he saw the cruel nails driven through hands and feet, and the blows that broke the skin, tore the flesh and crushed the bones and let out the life's blood of his Son. He looked upon that.

''In the case of our Father, the knife was not stayed, but it fell, and the life's blood of his beloved Son went out. His Father looked on with great grief and agony over his beloved Son, until there seems to have come a moment when even our Savior cried out in despair: 'My God, my God, why hast thou forsaken me?'

''In that hour I think I can see our dear Father behind the veil looking upon these dying struggles until even he could not endure it any longer; and, like the mother who bids farewell to her dying child, has to be taken out of the room, so as not to look upon the last struggles, so he bowed his head, and hid in some part of his universe, his great heart almost breaking for the love that he had for his Son.

''Oh, in that moment when he might have saved his Son, I thank him and praise him that he did not fail us, for he had not only the love of his Son in mind, but he had love for us, and I rejoice that he did not interfere, and that his love for us made it possible for him to endure to look upon the sufferings of his Son and give him finally to us, our Savior and our Redeemer. For without him, without his sacrifice, we would have been buried in the earth, and there our bodies would have remained and we would never have come glorified into his presence. And so this is what it cost, in part, for our Father in heaven to give the gift of his Son unto men.'' (*Improvement Era*, October 1919, pp. 1029-31.)

In early Christian times, some of the converts put private interpretations upon this event and went far afield. Most of them were Jews who venerated Abraham anyway. They endeavored to mix the Abrahamic story with the account of Jesus on the cross, and made a combined presentation of two great sacrifices in the holy eucharist. Artwork also began to appear then, working the Abrahamic story into the atonement of Christ. But the difficulty in such a procedure was soon recognized and the matter was stopped.

The place of the sacrifice was on Mount Moriah, which later became the site for the erection of the temple of Solomon. This was also where the Lord appeared to David. (2 Chronicles 3:1.) A giant mosque is now upon this place, evidencing the great respect the Arabs have for their illustrious ancestor.

Chapter 29

THE MARRIAGE COVENANT

One of the great lessons we find in the life of Abraham is his strict adherence to the marriage covenant and the requirement that we marry within the faith and within the race.

How devastated he would have been if Isaac had married a Canaanite!

Abraham remembered that he had relatives in Haran where he had left his father, and to which area his brother Nahor afterward moved. He desired that one of the women of that branch of the family become the wife of Isaac.

The Lord too desired that Isaac marry well for the covenant's sake. Jesus Christ would be born in that lineage. The bloodline must be kept pure.

Abraham had a trusted servant and decided to send him to the home of Nahor for a daughter to marry Isaac. So careful was Abraham in this matter that he put his servant under oath. The scripture reads:

"And Abraham was old, and well stricken in age: and the Lord had blessed Abraham in all things.

"And Abraham said unto his eldest servant of his house, that ruled over all that he had, Put, I pray thee, thy hand under my thigh:

"And I will make thee swear by the Lord, the God of heaven, and the God of the earth, that thou shalt not take a wife unto my son of the daughters of the Canaanites, among whom I dwell:

"But thou shalt go unto my country, and to my kindred, and take a wife unto my son Isaac. . . .

"And the servant put his hand under the thigh of Abraham his master, and sware to him concerning that matter.

"And the servant took ten camels of the camels of his master, and departed; for all the goods of his master were in his hand: and he arose, and went to Mesopotamia, unto the city of Nahor." (Genesis 24:1-4, 9-10.)

The rest of the story is told in Genesis. Isaac married Rebekah, within the family line.

The relationship of Isaac and Rebekah is given in this way: "And I bowed down my head, and worshipped the Lord, and blessed the Lord God of my master Abraham, which had led me in the right way to take my master's brother's daughter unto his son." (Genesis 24:48.)

The "master's brother" was Nahor, with whom Abraham was reared in Ur.

The same kind of caution was shown in the selection of a bride for Jacob. Again the bloodline was chosen. Again the lineage was kept pure, looking to the Savior's birth.

The same caution was pressed upon the Israelites in the days of Moses. Realizing that there were many unbelievers in the land, and that most of the neighbors were Canaanites, the Lord prohibited mixed marriages with them.

Among his declarations was the following:

"Neither shalt thou make marriages with them; thy daughter thou shalt not give unto his son, nor his daughter shalt thou take unto thy son.

"For they will turn away thy son from following me, that they may serve other gods: so will the anger of the Lord be kindled against you, and destroy thee suddenly. . . .

"The Lord did not set his love upon you, nor choose you, because ye were more in number than any people; for ye were the fewest of all people." (Deuteronomy 7:3-4, 7.)

At another time the Lord decreed:

"This is the thing which the Lord doth command concerning the daughters of Zelophehad, saying, Let them marry to whom they think best; only to the family of the tribe of their father shall they marry.

"So shall not the inheritance of the children of Israel remove from tribe to tribe: for every one of the children of Israel shall keep himself to the inheritance of the tribe of his fathers.

"And every daughter, that possesseth an inheritance in any tribe of the children of Israel, shall be wife unto one of the family of the tribe of her father, that the children of Israel may enjoy every man the inheritance of his fathers." (Numbers 36:6-8.)

Among the Latter-day Saints, the Lord provides temple marriage, which, of course, limits participation to the believers.

Chapter 30

ABRAHAM'S ASTRONOMY

The Lord seems to have taken pleasure in revealing to his ancient prophets the wonders of the heavens, the planets, and the great organizations that support them.

He unveiled his creations to Abraham, and showed them in great detail to Moses. Those early prophets knew about the movement of the sun, moon, and stars, and understood how they were controlled. The idea that the world was flat is something that never occurred to them, nor that the sun moved around the earth, which some at times have believed. They did not partake of the ignorance that characterized many other peoples.

When the *Reader's Digest* published an atlas of the world, the editors introduced it with a preface telling of the beliefs and superstitions of men before the genuine facts became available. This atlas quoted people of the dark ages as saying: "Paradise is somewhere in the Far East. Jerusalem is the center of all nations and countries, and the world itself is a flat disk surrounded by oceans of water."

The publishers then went on to provide in contrast colored maps and pictures of various parts of the world, revealing that the earth is a globe and is but a minor part of vast creations in the heavens.

Ancient prophets knew that our solar system was but a small part of the vast creations of God in which there were many planets and stars. They knew that creation goes on and on, and that there is no space in which there is not a "kingdom." "And as one earth shall pass away, and the heavens thereof even so shall another come, and there is no end to my works, neither to my words." (Moses 1:38.)

Abraham "saw the stars, that they were very great, and that one of them was nearest unto the throne of God; and there were many great ones which were near unto it." (Abraham 3:2.)

As he showed Abraham the vastness of creation, with all the

stars and other heavenly bodies, he stated that his purpose was to give Abraham a posterity as numerous as these. (Abraham 3:14.)

Abraham possessed the Urim and Thummim. The Lord had given it to him while he was yet in Ur. Through it he not only received the word of God, but it also became an instrument through which the Lord revealed to him the secrets of the skies. He studied the stars with God himself as the instructor.

"And the Lord said unto me: These are the governing ones; and the name of the great one is Kolob, because it is near unto me, for I am the Lord thy God: I have set this one to govern all those which belong to the same order as that upon which thou standest.

"And the Lord said unto me, by the Urim and Thummim, that Kolob was after the manner of the Lord, according to its times and seasons in the revolutions thereof; that one revolution was a day unto the Lord, after his manner of reckoning, it being one thousand years according to the time appointed unto that whereon thou standest. This is the reckoning of the Lord's time, according to the reckoning of Kolob." (Abraham 3:3-4.)

The planet Kolob became of great interest to Abraham. The Lord explained that it "is set nigh unto the throne of God" and that it governs "all those planets which belong to the same order as that upon which thou standest." (Abraham 3:9.)

It is interesting to note that the throne of God is on a separate planet in the sky, with Kolob being nearby.

Reference made here to the planets of the same order as this earth is enlightening in view of other scriptures. In a revelation to the Prophet Joseph Smith, we have this:

"All kingdoms have a law given;

"And there are many kingdoms; for there is no space in the which there is no kingdom; and there is no kingdom in which there is no space, either a greater or a lesser kingdom.

"And unto every kingdom is given a law; and unto every law there are certain bounds also and conditions." (D&C 88:36-38.)

As our hymn by W. W. Phelps says:

> The works of God continue,
> And worlds and lives abound;
> Improvement and progression
> Have one eternal round.

There is no end to matter;
There is no end to space;
There is no end to spirit;
There is no end to race.
—*Hymns*, no. 257

Moses, too, was shown the vastness of creation, as indeed was Enoch. When Moses described what he saw he wrote:

"And behold, the glory of the Lord was upon Moses, so that Moses stood in the presence of God, and talked with him face to face. And the Lord God said unto Moses: For mine own purpose have I made these things. Here is wisdom and it remaineth in me.

"And by the word of my power, have I created them, which is mine Only Begotten Son, who is full of grace and truth.

"And worlds without number have I created; and I also created them for mine own purpose; and by the Son I created them, which is mine Only Begotten." (Moses 1:31-33.)

And Enoch said: "And were it possible that man could number the particles of the earth, yea, millions of earths like this, is would not be a beginning to the number of thy creations; and thy curtains are stretched out still; and yet thou art there, and thy bosom is there; and also thou art just; thou art merciful and kind forever." (Moses 7:30.)

The Book of Mormon people knew about the stars and their movements, and they understood about the sun "standing still" in the days of Joshua. Says Helaman: "Yea, if he [God] say unto the earth—Thou shalt go back, that it lengthen out the day for many hours—it is done; And thus, according to his word the earth goeth back, and it appeareth unto man that the sun standeth still; yea, and behold, this is so; for surely it is the earth that moveth and not the sun." (Helaman 12:14-15.)

It is clear, then, that these early Americans knew about the movement of the heavenly orbs. Archaeology has proven this.

When the prophets were shown the heavens, one thing was made certain and clear: *God created them all.* The doctrine of a divine creation was no problem to them, and it never will be to believers in the revelations.

Are there other planets which are inhabited? The answer to that, of course, is affirmative, as we read in the Doctrine and Covenants:

"And now, after the many testimonies which have been given of him, this is the testimony, last of all, which we give of him: That he lives!

"For we saw him, even on the right hand of God; and we heard the voice bearing record that he is the Only Begotten of the Father—

"That by him, and through him, and of him, the worlds are and were created, and the inhabitants thereof are begotten sons and daughters unto God." (D&C 76:22-24.)

No doubt many other earths are mortal like ours and have on them human beings like ourselves. They must look like us because we are all the children of God and he made us all in his image.

The May 1978 issue of the magazine of the Smithsonian Institution features an article on possible life in space, written by Dr. Carl Sagan, director of Cornell University's Laboratory for Planetary Studies. He begins his article by saying: "Through all of our history we have pondered the stars and mused whether mankind is unique or if, somewhere else out there in the dark of the night sky, there are other beings who contemplate and wonder as we do, fellow thinkers in the cosmos."

He does not stop to discuss the kind of microscopic life other scientists are searching for, both here and on Mars, but do not find. He talks in terms of intelligent adult life that may enjoy "advanced technical civilizations" on these other orbs. He looks at our Milky Way galaxy and estimates that among the 250 billion stars in that formation, there probably are a million planets that support advanced civilizations.

Serious efforts are presently being made to communicate with possible life "out there." Dr. Sagan mentions eight such programs being conducted by the United States, Canada, and the Soviet Union. Since he estimates that there may be intelligent civilized life on a million planets in our galaxy, what does the rest of creation have to offer? As we contemplate such things, we can begin to understand in some degree the infinitude of God.

Most likely there are many orbs on which dwell people who already have passed through mortality. It is certain that we who belong to this earth will eventually occupy such eternal homes as resurrected persons.

Paul spoke of this in his epistle to the Corinthians:

"There are also celestial bodies, and bodies terrestrial: but the glory of the celestial is one, and the glory of the terrestrial is another.

"There is one glory of the sun, and another glory of the moon, and another glory of the stars: for one star differeth from another star in glory.

"So also is the resurrection of the dead. It is sown in corruption; it is raised in incorruption." (1 Corinthians 15:40-42.)

Section 76 of the Doctrine and Covenants makes this doctrine clear. What section 88 tells us is also remarkable. First the Lord speaks there of the earth itself being celestialized. Then he tells us concerning the people who will occupy it after the resurrection:

"Now, verily I say unto you, that through the redemption which is made for you is brought to pass the resurrection from the dead.

"And the spirit and the body are the soul of man.

"And the resurrection from the dead is the redemption of the soul.

"And the redemption of the soul is through him that quickeneth all things, in whose bosom it is decreed that the poor and the meek of the earth shall inherit it.

"Therefore, it must needs be sanctified from all unrighteousness, that it may be prepared for the celestial glory;

"For after it hath filled the measure of its creation, it shall be crowned with glory, even with the presence of God the Father;

"That bodies who are of the celestial kingdom may possess it forever and ever; for, for this intent was it made and created, and for this intent are they sanctified.

"And they who are not sanctified through the law which I have given unto you, even the law of Christ, must inherit another kingdom, even that of a terrestrial kingdom, or that of a telestial kingdom.

"For he who is not able to abide the law of a celestial kingdom cannot abide a celestial glory.

"And he who cannot abide the law of a terrestrial kingdom cannot abide a terrestrial glory.

"And he who cannot abide the law of a telestial kingdom

cannot abide a telestial glory; therefore he is not meet for a kingdom of glory. Therefore he must abide a kingdom which is not a
kingdom of glory.

"And again, verily I say unto you, the earth abideth the law
of a celestial kingdom, for it filleth the measure of its creation,
and transgresseth not the law—

"Wherefore, it shall be sanctified; yea, notwithstanding it
shall die, it shall be quickened again, and shall abide the power
by which it is quickened, and the righteous shall inherit it.

"For notwithstanding they die, they also shall rise again, a
spiritual body.

"They who are of a celestial spirit shall receive the same
body which was a natural body; even ye shall receive your
bodies, and your glory shall be that glory by which your bodies
are quickened.

"Ye who are quickened by a portion of the celestial glory
shall then receive of the same, even a fulness.

"And they who are quickened by a portion of the terrestrial
glory shall then receive of the same, even a fulness.

"And also they who are quickened by a portion of the telestial glory shall then receive of the same, even a fulness.

"And they who remain shall also be quickened; nevertheless,
they shall return again to their own place, to enjoy that which
they are willing to receive, because they were not willing to enjoy
that which they might have received." (D&C 88:14-32.)

After the resurrection, the planets to be occupied by the redeemed apparently will be in new orbits, in separate classified
areas of space. Their locations are not revealed. But is it not of
great importance to learn that the earth will become like a giant
Urim and Thummim in its celestialized state?

"In answer to the question—Is not the reckoning of God's
time, angel's time, prophet's time, and man's time, according to
the planet on which they reside?

"I answer, Yes. But there are no angels who minister to this
earth but those who do belong or have belonged to it.

"The angels do not reside on a planet like this earth;

"But they reside in the presence of God, on a globe like a sea
of glass and fire, where all things for their glory are manifest,
past, present, and future, and are continually before the Lord.

"The place where God resides is a great Urim and Thummim.

"This earth, in its sanctified and immortal state, will be made like unto crystal and will be a Urim and Thummim to the inhabitants who dwell thereon, whereby all things pertaining to an inferior kingdom, or all kingdoms of a lower order, will be manifest to those who dwell on it; and this earth will be Christ's.

"Then the white stone mentioned in Revelation 2:17, will become a Urim and Thummim to each individual who receives one, whereby things pertaining to a higher order of kingdoms will be made known." (D&C 130:4-10.)

Elder Parley P. Pratt, a member of the Council of Twelve in the days of the Prophet Joseph Smith, also wrote of the many worlds:

"All these kingdoms, with all their intelligences . . . are so many colonies of our race, multiplied, extended, transplanted, and existing for ever and ever, as occupants of the numberless planetary systems that do now exist or that will roll into order and be peopled by the operations of the Holy Spirit in obedience to the mandates of the sons of God.

"These kingdoms present every variety and degree in the progress of the great science of life, from the lowest degradation amid the realms of death, or the rudimental states of elementary existence, upward through all the ascending scale or all the degrees of progress in the science of eternal life and light, until some of them in turn rise to thrones of eternal power. . . .

"The earth and other systems are to undergo a variety of changes in their progress toward perfection. . . .

"A new heaven and a new earth are promised by the sacred writers. Or, in other words, the planetary systems are to be changed, purified, refined, exalted, and glorified, in the similitude of the resurrection, by which means all physical evil or imperfection will be done away. . . .

"When man and the planet on which he lives, with all its fulness, shall have completed all their series of progressive changes so as to be adapted to the highest glories of which their several characters and species are capable, then the whole will be annexed to or numbered with the eternal heavens, and will there fulfil their eternal rounds, being another acquisition to the mansions or eternally increasing dominions of the great Creator and Redeemer.'' (*Key to the Science of Theology*, Deseret Book Company, 1978 edition, pp. 22, 34-35.)

Interestingly enough, President Brigham Young said this about our research into astronomy:

''Mankind have degenerated; they have lost the physical and mental power they once possessed. In many points pertaining to mechanism, men have in modern times been instructed by revelation to them, and this mechanical knowledge causes them almost to boast against their Creator, and to set themselves up as competitors with the Lord Almighty, notwithstanding they have produced nothing but what has been revealed to them.

''In the knowledge of astronomical and other philosophical truths, which our modern great men are searching after and pride themselves in, they are but babes, compared with the ancient fathers. Do the wise men of modern ages understand the laws which govern the worlds that are, that were, and that are to come? They cannot fathom this matter. They have grown weaker when they ought to have grown stronger and wiser.'' (*Discourses of Brigham Young*, p. 106.)

As yet our greatest researchers have hardly begun to learn about astronomy. Not only are there those countless orbs in their present state, but there will also be an entirely new field of knowledge and experience awaiting those who will be redeemed from mortality and will then reach their final eternal state.

Is that what John the Revelator saw when he wrote: ''And I saw a new heaven and a new earth: for the first heaven and the first earth were passed away; and there was no more sea''? (Revelation 21:1.)

Peter also spoke of it in these words: ''Nevertheless we, according to his promise, look for new heavens and a new earth, wherein dwelleth righteousness.'' (2 Peter 3:13.)

As W. W. Phelps further expressed himself:

> There is no end to glory;
> There is no end to love;
> There is no end to being;
> There is no death above.

Chapter 31

THE DEATH OF SARAH

Sarah was ninety years old when Isaac was born. She lived on until she reached the age of 127; then she died in Hebron, in the land of Canaan. "And Abraham came to mourn for Sarah, and to weep for her." (Genesis 23:1-2.)

As a stranger in a strange land, he sought for a suitable place for her burial. He came to the sons of Heth and said:

"I am a stranger and a sojourner with you: give me a possession of a buryingplace with you, that I may bury my dead out of my sight.

"And the children of Heth answered Abraham, saying unto him,

"Hear us, my lord: thou art a mighty prince among us: in the choice of our sepulchres bury thy dead; none of us shall withhold from thee his sepulchre, but that thou mayest bury thy dead.

"And Abraham stood up, and bowed himself to the people of the land, even to the children of Heth.

"And he communed with them, saying, If it be your mind that I should bury my dead out of my sight; hear me, and intreat for me to Ephron the son of Zohar,

"That he may give me the cave of Machpelah, which he hath, which is in the end of his field; for as much money as it is worth he shall give it me for a possession of a buryingplace amongst you.

"And Ephron dwelt among the children of Heth: and Ephron the Hittite answered Abraham in the audience of the children of Heth, even of all that went in at the gate of his city, saying,

"Nay, my lord, hear me: the field give I thee, and the cave that is therein, I give it thee; in the presence of the sons of my people give I it thee: bury thy dead.

"And Abraham bowed down himself before the people of the land.

"And he spake unto Ephron in the audience of the people of the land, saying, But if thou wilt give it, I pray thee, hear me: I will give thee money for the field; take it of me, and I will bury my dead there.

"And Ephron answered Abraham, saying unto him,

"My lord, hearken unto me: the land is worth four hundred shekels of silver; what is that betwixt me and thee? bury therefore thy dead.

"And Abraham hearkened unto Ephron; and Abraham weighed to Ephron the silver, which he had named in the audience of the sons of Heth, four hundred shekels of silver, current money with the merchant.

"And the field of Ephron, which was in Machpelah, which was before Mamre, the field, and the cave which was therein, and all the trees that were in the field, that were in all the borders round about, were made sure.

"Unto Abraham for a possession in the presence of the children of Heth, before all that went in at the gate of his city.

"And after this, Abraham buried Sarah his wife in the cave of the field of Machpelah before Mamre: the same is Hebron in the land of Canaan.

"And the field, and the cave that is therein, were made sure unto Abraham for a possession of a buryingplace by the sons of Heth." (Genesis 23:4-20.)

Following the death of Sarah, Abraham was married again, this time to Keturah, and by her he had more children. No further mention is made of Hagar.

When Abraham was "stricken in years," and very old, he divided his estate among his children. He "gave all that he had unto Isaac.

"But unto the sons of the concubines, which Abraham had, Abraham gave gifts, and sent them away from Isaac his son, while he yet lived, eastward, unto the east country.

"And these are the days of the years of Abraham's life which he lived, an hundred threescore and fifteen years.

"Then Abraham gave up the ghost, and died in a good old age, an old man, and full of years; and was gathered to his people.

"And his sons Isaac and Ishmael buried him in the cave of

Machpelah, in the field of Ephron the son of Zohar the Hittite, which is before Mamre;

"The field which Abraham purchased of the sons of Heth: there was Abraham buried, and Sarah his wife." (Genesis 25:5-10.)

Both Isaac and Ishmael participated in his burial services. Again, no mention is made of Hagar.

Abraham, the Friend of God, was faithful in all things. When the Lord spoke to the Prophet Joseph about him, it was revealed that Abraham is now in resurrected glory and has received his exaltation. Said the Lord: "Abraham received all things, whatsoever he received, by revelation and commandment, by my word, saith the Lord, and hath entered into his exaltation and sitteth upon his throne." (D&C 132:29.)

Chapter 32

THE BOOK
OF ABRAHAM

The Book of Abraham is one of our most important volumes of scripture. Consider for a moment what it provides:

1. It shows us the process by which Jehovah was chosen to be the Savior of this world.

2. It gives us a glimpse into the premortal life, our life before we came into mortality.

3. It explains how God's leaders in this world were selected in the pre-earth life, since they were also leaders in that pristine period.

4. It provides a remarkable description of the creation by "the Gods," showing a plurality of Personages engaged therein.

5. It gives us a divinely inspired lesson in astronomy, as taught by the Lord himself. Abraham was shown the vast creations in the heavens, with the Almighty himself making the explanations, for creation came about by divine action.

6. It also adds some history concerning the early life of Abraham, his relationship to God, and a further understanding of the divine promises made to that ancient patriarch.

Most people who believe in Christ are of the opinion that the Lord's career began with his birth in Bethlehem on that first Christmas night. There is little reason for them to think such a thing, for the Bible clearly shows that Jesus had a premortal life wherein he achieved Godhood. (John 1:1-14; Hebrews 1:1-3.)

Jesus was chosen to be the Savior before this world was made. But how was he chosen for this great honor? Two mortal men that we know of were shown some details of this significant event. They were Abraham and Moses.

Abraham was shown the premortal spirits who were leaders among the primeval family of God. Of this he wrote:

"Now the Lord had shown unto me, Abraham, the intelligences that were organized before the world was; and among all these there were many of the noble and great ones;

"And God saw these souls that they were good, and he stood in the midst of them, and he said: These I will make my rulers; for he stood among those that were spirits, and he saw that they were good; and he said unto me: Abraham, thou art one of them; thou wast chosen before thou wast born.

"And there stood one among them that was like unto God, and he said unto those who were with him: We will go down, for there is space there, and we will take of these materials, and we will make an earth whereon these may dwell;

"And we will prove them herewith, to see if they will do all things whatsoever the Lord their God shall command them;

"And they who keep their first estate shall be added upon; and they who keep not their first estate shall not have glory in the same kingdom with those who keep their first estate; and they who keep their second estate shall have glory added upon their heads for ever and ever." (Abraham 3:22-26.)

These were the spirit children of God, especially those who were to become leaders on earth, since evidently they already were leaders in the premortal world.

In particular was Abraham shown the Savior. He wrote: "And there stood one among them that was like unto God." (Abraham 3:24.)

There is only one Personage "like unto God," and that is Jesus the Christ, who at that pristine period was Jehovah. (D&C 110:1-4.)

How did John describe him? As being with God, and as a God himself, the Creator, for "all things were made by him; and without him was not any thing made that was made." (John 1:1-3.)

Paul described him as being "like unto God" when he told the Colossians that he was the image of the "invisible God, the firstborn of every creature:

"For by him were all things created, that are in heaven, and that are in earth, visible and invisible, whether they be thrones, or dominions, or principalities, or powers: all things were created by him, and for him:

"And he is before all things, and by him all things consist.

"And he is the head of the body, the church: who is the beginning, the firstborn from the dead; that in all things he might have the preeminence.

"For it pleased the Father that in him should all fulness dwell." (Colossians 1:15-19.)

Paul also told the Hebrews that Christ was the "express image" of his Father's person. (Hebrews 1:3.)

And, of course, the Savior taught his disciples that whoever had seen him had seen the Father, indicating that each was in the "express image" of the other. (John 12:45; 14:9.)

It is noted that our premortal life was spoken of as our "first estate" and that our earth life was referred to as our "second estate." The promise was there given that if the spirits who kept their first estate would also keep their second estate, that is, live righteously and successfully here on earth, they would then be "added upon" with glory "for ever and ever."

And then Abraham reveals the selection of the Savior: "And the Lord said: Whom shall I send? And one answered like unto the Son of Man: Here am I, send me. And another answered and said: Here am I, send me. And the Lord said: I will send the first." (Abraham 3:27.)

In that early council two volunteered to save the world, but only one was chosen. The other was rebellious and "kept not his first estate." He fought against God, and "at that day, many followed after him." (Abraham 3:28.) He became Satan.

Moses wrote of this same event:

"And I, the Lord God, spake unto Moses, saying: That Satan, whom thou hast commanded in the name of mine Only Begotten, is the same which was from the beginning, and he came before me, saying—Behold, here am I, send me, I will be thy son, and I will redeem all mankind, that one soul shall not be lost, and surely I will do it; wherefore give me thine honor.

"But, behold, my Beloved Son, which was my Beloved and Chosen from the beginning, said unto me—Father, thy will be done, and the glory be thine forever.

"Wherefore, because that Satan rebelled against me, and sought to destroy the agency of man, which I, the Lord God, had given him, and also, that I should give unto him mine own power; by the power of mine Only Begotten, I caused that he should be cast down;

"And he became Satan, yea, even the devil, the father of all lies, to deceive and to blind men, and to lead them captive at his will, even as many as would not hearken unto my voice." (Moses 4:1-4.)

The fall of Satan was also shown to Joseph Smith who wrote of that event in this language:

"And this we saw also, and bear record, that an angel of God who was in authority in the presence of God, who rebelled against the Only Begotten Son whom the Father loved and who was in the bosom of the Father, was thrust down from the presence of God and the Son,

"And was called Perdition, for the heavens wept over him—he was Lucifer, a son of the morning.

"And we beheld, and lo, he is fallen! is fallen, even a son of the morning!

"And while we were yet in the Spirit, the Lord commanded us that we should write the vision; for we beheld Satan, that old serpent, even the devil, who rebelled against God, and sought to take the kingdom of our God and his Christ—

"Wherefore, he maketh war with the saints of God, and encompasseth them round about.

"And we saw a vision of the sufferings of those with whom he made war and overcame, for thus came the voice of the Lord unto us." (D&C 76:25-30.)

John the Revelator was shown details of this event also and recorded:

"And there was war in heaven: Michael and his angels fought against the dragon; and the dragon fought and his angels,

"And prevailed not; neither was their place found any more in heaven.

"And the great dragon was cast out, that old serpent, called the Devil, and Satan, which deceiveth the whole world: he was cast out into the earth, and his angels were cast out with him." (Revelation 12:7-9.)

Isaiah also spoke of the fall of this "son of the morning":

"How art thou fallen from heaven, O Lucifer, son of the morning! how art thou cut down to the ground, which didst weaken the nations!

"For thou hast said in thine heart, I will ascend into heaven, I will exalt my throne above the stars of God: I will sit also upon the mount of the congregation, in the sides of the north:

"I will ascend above the heights of the clouds; I will be like the most High.

"Yet thou shalt be brought down to hell, to the sides of the pit." (Isaiah 14:12-15.)

It will be noted in Moses' record of these events that Lucifer said: "Behold, here am I, send me, I will be thy son, and I will redeem all mankind, that one soul shall not be lost, and surely I will do it; wherefore give me thine honor." (Moses 4:1.)

Here is illustrated two dreadful things: One was the unmitigated and colossal egotism of Lucifer. The other was his determination to save people by force "that one soul shall not be lost." He would have destroyed free agency and thus made slaves of us all, his slaves, forever doomed to obey his wicked commands.

It is no wonder that the scripture says of him: "And he became Satan, yea, even the devil, the father of all lies, to deceive and to blind men, and to lead them captive at his will, even as many as would not hearken unto my voice." (Moses 4:4.)

From these scriptures it is evident that our Father in heaven intended that indeed the Savior, chosen in the premortal life to come here and offer salvation to all, would actually be his Son, the Son of God.

What a beautiful expression he made in that primeval council: "But, behold, my Beloved Son, which was my Beloved and Chosen from the beginning, said unto me—Father, thy will be done, and the glory be thine forever." (Moses 4:2.) The Lord's prayer in Gethsemane was but a reflection of this same attitude.

So Jehovah was not only the Father's firstborn in the spirit world, but when he came to earth, he also became the only Begotten in the flesh. Thus on that first Christmas night, he became "Emmanuel, which being interpreted is, God with us." (Matthew 1:23.) Thus he became "the Son of the Highest," inheriting the throne "of his father David." (Luke 1:32.) And thus his name on earth was divinely called Jesus, "for he shall save his people from their sins." (Matthew 1:21.)

Jesus the Christ! Or as John the Baptist knew him, "The Lamb of God, which taketh away the sin of the world." (John 1:29.)

So it was also that even to the Samaritan woman who spoke of the expected Christ, he said: "I that speak unto thee am he." (John 4:26.)

He organized his church, through which salvation comes. The Saints who are faithful therein are "they who are the church of the Firstborn. They are they into whose hands the Father has given all things." (D&C 76:54-55.)

To Abraham was revealed the selection of the Savior, and he recorded it for us to read.

The Book of Abraham, like the Book of Moses, is rich in doctrine and abundant in revealed facts so vital to our welfare. It is revelation. It is scripture. We accept it as we do others of our standard works. It is an essential part of the sacred literature of The Church of Jesus Christ of Latter-day Saints.

Chapter 33

ABRAHAM ON CREATION

The account of creation as given in the Book of Abraham is distinctive in that it says that great work was done by ''the Gods'' in contrast to the belief that one God—one Almighty Being—made all things by himself, and out of nothing. There was a plurality of Gods engaged in creation. This fact is well corroborated in the Bible, including some passages in Genesis.

The Book of Abraham definitely teaches that this earth was made purposely as a home for the spirit offspring of God. It was not something that came about through some big accidental ''bang,'' as the scientists say. Neither is life something that sprang up spontaneously and ''grew like Topsy'' with neither rhyme nor reason, spreading out into all its species.

God had space available. He had materials from which to make an earth, and he used them in his creative work. He did not make it out of nothing.

Most of his spirit children had kept their first estate. Now he was ready to introduce them to a second estate. ''And we will prove them herewith to see if they will do all things whatsoever the Lord their God shall command them.'' So he said, ''We will make an earth whereon these may dwell.'' (Abraham 3:25, 24.) This reveals the purpose in creation.

Thus earth life became a testing time, to see ''if they will do all things whatsoever the Lord their God shall command them.''

But what a reward if they will be faithful! ''They who keep their second estate shall have glory added upon their heads for ever and ever.'' (Abraham 3:26.) And ''all that my Father hath shall be given'' unto them. (D&C 84:38.)

So it was with this purpose that the Lord said: ''Let us go down. And they went down at the beginning, and they, that is the Gods, organized and formed the heavens and the earth.'' (Abraham 4:1.)

It was not a matter of making an earth—or the heavens—out of nothing. They went down and organized the materials that were available in space that also was available, and thus they provided creation.

"And the earth, after it was formed, was empty and desolate, because they had not formed anything but the earth; and darkness reigned upon the face of the deep, and the Spirit of the Gods was brooding upon the face of the waters." (Abraham 4:2.)

Note that not only were the Gods in conversation while employed in this creative undertaking, but "the Spirit of the Gods was brooding upon the face of the waters."

Then how was creation brought about? How were these materials organized into an earth? By the power of the Spirit of the Gods working under the direction of the Gods!

Mankind at times has seen but slight expressions of the powers of so-called nature. Earthquakes have shaken large areas, even changed their shape. Floods have come, lightning has struck with death and destruction, and tidal waves have devastated the land. Would not such powers of nature have been employed in forming and organizing the earth?

Who were these Gods?

We believe in a Godhead of Father, Son, and Holy Ghost. Who else would have participated in the creation?

Moses quoted the Lord in his revelation of the creation as saying: "And by the word of my power, have I created them, which is mine Only Begotten Son, who is full of grace and truth. And worlds without number have I created; and I also created them for mine own purpose; and by the Son I created them, which is mine Only Begotten." (Moses 1:32-33.)

The apostle Paul gave this same view to the Hebrews as he wrote:

"God, who at sundry times and in divers manners spake in time past unto the fathers by the prophets,

"Hath in these last days spoken unto us by his Son, whom he hath appointed heir of all things, *by whom also he made the worlds*;

"Who being the brightness of his glory, and the express image of his person, and upholding all things by the word of his power, when he had by himself purged our sins, sat down on the right hand of the Majesty on high.'' (Hebrews 1:1-3. Italics added.)

When John wrote his gospel he said: ''In the beginning was the Word, and the Word was with God, and the Word was God. The same was in the beginning with God. All things were made by him; and without him was not any thing made that was made.'' (John 1:1-3.)

Some of the newer translations of the Bible read as follows:

The *New English Bible*: ''When all things began, the Word already was. The Word dwelt with God, and what God was, the Word was. The Word, then, was with God at the beginning, and through him all things came to be; no single thing was created without him.''

The *Authentic New Testament* (Schonfield): ''In the beginning was the Word. And the Word was with God. So the Word was divine. He was in the beginning with God. By him everything had being. And without him nothing had being. What had being by him was Life. And Life was the Light of men.''

The *New World Translation*: ''In the beginning the Word was, and the Word was with God, and the Word was a god. This one was in the beginning with God. All things came into existence through him, and apart from him not even one thing came into existence.''

Knox Roman Catholic Version: ''At the beginning of time the Word already was; and God had the Word abiding with him, and the Word was God. He abode, at the beginning of time, with God. It was through him that all things came into being, and without him came nothing that has come to be.''

Goodspeed American Translation: ''In the beginning the Word existed. The Word was with God, and the Word was divine. It was he that was with God in the beginning. Everything came into existence through him, and apart from him nothing came to be.''

When Abraham's revelation of the Creation discussed details, it is interesting that he used such expressions as these: ''And the Gods prepared the earth to bring forth the living creature after his kind,'' ''And the Gods organized the earth to bring forth the beasts after their kind,'' ''And the Gods took counsel among themselves and said, Let us go down and form man in our image.''

It is obvious that there was a plurality of Creators who worked together, and that they counseled and planned their work in advance.

The plural nature of the participation in creation is borne out in passages in the King James Translation. For example, Genesis 1:26 reads: "And God said, Let *us* make man in *our* image." (Italics added.) Note the plural form.

When the devil tempted Eve he said: "Ye shall be as gods, knowing good and evil." (Genesis 3:5.) What Gods? And after the fall, "The Lord God said, Behold, the man is become as one of *us*." (Italics added.) (Genesis 3:22.) Note again the plural form.

The Roman Catholic *Jerusalem Bible* reads, regarding the creation of man: "God said, Let *us* make man in *our* image." (Italics added.)

The *Knox Bible* says: "And God said, Let *us* make man wearing *our* image." (Italics added.) Other Bibles say essentially the same.

After the fall, the versions read:

Knox: "Here is Adam become like one of *ourselves*." (Italics added.)

Goodspeed: "Man has become like one of *us* in knowing good and evil." (Italics added.)

Joseph Smith's Translation: "And I, the Lord God, said unto mine Only Begotten, Behold, the man is become as one of us, to know good and evil." (JST Genesis 3:28.)

Here is the answer: God spoke to his Beloved Son, and as we read these words, we see that the scriptures make sense in giving the plural form in each case.

Like Moses, Abraham was not present as an eyewitness to creation so that he could write about it first hand. He obtained all this detail in only one way—by revelation, just as Moses did.

In the case of the Book of Moses, the revelation given to Moses comprising that book was again given as modern revelation to the Prophet Joseph Smith, and notations to that effect appear at the heads of the chapters of that book. The Book of Abraham has no such designations, but it could only be by revelation that this intimate picture of creation was provided.

The Prophet Joseph Smith, as is well known, obtained ancient writings in Egyptian mummies that he purchased. He makes frequent reference to them, one as the book of Abraham and the other as the book of Joseph, who was sold into Egypt.

President Joseph Fielding Smith wrote of this in his book *Essentials in Church History*:

"On the 3rd of July, 1835, Michael H. Chandler, came to Kirtland exhibiting four mummies and some rolls of papyrus covered with hieroglyphic figures. Mr. Chandler had been directed to the Prophet Joseph Smith as one who could translate the characters for him. At his request Joseph Smith gave a translation of a few of them which Mr. Chandler stated agreed with the decipherings of learned men who had examined them. He gave the Prophet a certificate to this effect. Shortly after this interview some of the Saints in Kirtland purchased the mummies and the manuscripts, and, with Oliver Cowdery and Wm. W. Phelps as scribes, the Prophet commenced to translate these records. To their great joy they discovered that one of these rolls contained writings of Abraham, or instructions given to him in Egypt from the Lord. The other contained writings of Joseph, son of Jacob. During the summer the Prophet prepared for the complete translation of the Book of Abraham, as it is called, which now appears in the Pearl of Great Price, one of the accepted standard works of the Church." (Pp. 183-84.)

In his historical writings, the Prophet speaks of these ancient records from time to time. Some of his references are as follows:

"Soon after this, some of the Saints at Kirtland purchased the mummies and papyrus, a description of which will appear hereafter, and with W. W. Phelps and Oliver Cowdery as scribes, I commenced the translation of some of the characters or hieroglyphics, and much to our joy found that one of the rolls contained the writings of Abraham, another the writings of Joseph of Egypt, etc.,—a more full account of which will appear in its place, as I proceed to examine or unfold them. Truly we can say, the Lord is beginning to reveal the abundance of peace and truth." (HC 2:236.)

"This afternoon I labored on the Egyptian alphabet, in company with Brothers Oliver Cowdery and W. W. Phelps, and during the research, the principles of astronomy as understood by Father Abraham and the ancients unfolded to our understanding, the particulars of which will appear hereafter.'' (HC 2:286.)

"In the afternoon I waited on most of the Twelve, at my house, and exhibited to them the ancient records, and gave explanations. This day passed off with the blessing of the Lord.'' (HC 2:287.)

"I returned home and spent the day in translating the Egyptian records. . . . At home in the morning. Weather warm and rainy. We spent the day in translating, and made rapid progress.'' (HC 2:318.)

The book of Joseph was never published. Whether or not it was translated is not known.

Only fragments of the pieces of papyrus owned by the Prophet are now extant; most of what he had is now missing. Scholars believe that some of the few scraps of the ancient papyrus now in the possession of the Church are from documents other than the actual Book of Abraham, although the facsimiles now printed in the Pearl of Great Price are definitely from that original book.

However, the Book of Abraham as we publish it, containing the revelations of the Lord to Abraham, is indeed scripture and is invaluable. It was published by and with the full authority of the Prophet Joseph Smith, who gave it to us as translated scripture.

It appeared first in the *Times and Seasons* in Nauvoo beginning in March 1842, and later in the *Millennial Star* in England. The Prophet was assisted in this work by Elder Wilford Woodruff.

Several newspapers of the period gave repeated space to the work. The Boston *Daily Ledger* also published Facsimile No. 1, showing Abraham on the sacrificial altar, on the front page of its edition of Thursday, April 7, 1842. This facsimile was also published in the New York *Herald* and the *Dollar Week Bostonian*.

SCATTERED ISRAEL

When the Lord told Abraham that through his seed all the nations of the earth would be blessed, he had two things in mind.

One was that in his lineage the Savior would be born. All individuals and all peoples are blessed through his atonement and gospel teachings.

Second, through blood descent, all peoples would be blessed by lineage. But how could this be, when the family line was so restricted in the days of Isaac, Jacob, and his twelve sons? It was accomplished through the subsequent mixing of the blood of Israel among all nations as Israel was scattered.

The late Dr. James E. Talmage of the Council of the Twelve, writing in his *Articles of Faith*, described it in this way:

"It has been said, that 'if a complete history of the house of Israel were written, it would be the history of histories, the key of the world's history for the past twenty centuries.' Justification for this sweeping statement is found in the fact that the Israelites have been so completely dispersed among the nations as to give to this scattered people a place of importance as a factor in the rise and development of almost every large division of the human family. This work of dispersion was brought about by many stages, and extended through millenniums. It was foreseen by the early prophets; and the spiritual leaders of every generation prior to and immediately following the Messianic era predicted the scattering of the people, as an ordained result of their increasing wickedness, or referred to the fulfilment of former prophecies regarding the dispersion then already accomplished, and foretold a further and more complete diffusion of the nation." (Pp. 316-17.)

Various prophets in the Bible and Book of Mormon spoke of this scattering. As the Israelites mingled among the nations they intermarried, and thus their blood became a part of the peoples of the world. The coming of Lehi and his family to America was but one step in this scattering process.

Destruction came upon the nation of Israel in two steps. One was the capture and ultimate scattering of the Ten Tribes. The other was the scattering of the Jews following the destruction of Jerusalem in A.D. 70.

Dr. Talmage continues his description:

"Since the destruction of Jerusalem and the final disruption of the Jewish autonomy, the Jews have been wanderers upon the face of the earth, a people without a country, a nation without a home. The prophecy uttered by Amos of old has had its literal fulfilment—truly have Israel been sifted among all nations 'like as corn is sifted in a sieve.' Let it be remembered, however, that coupled with this dread prediction was the promise: 'Yet shall not the least grain fall upon the earth.' . . .

"As already stated, in the division of the Israelites after the death of Solomon ten tribes established themselves as an independent kingdom. This, the kingdom of Israel, was terminated as far as history is concerned by the Assyrian captivity, 721 B.C. The people were led into Assyria and later disappeared so completely that they have been called the Lost Tribes. They seem to have departed from Assyria, and while we lack definite information as to their final destination and present location, there is abundant evidence that their journey was toward the north. The Lord's word through Jeremiah promises that the people shall be brought back 'from the land of the north,' and a similar declaration has been made through divine revelation in the present dispensation.

"In the writings of Esdras or Ezra, which, however, are not included among the canonical books of the Bible but are known as apocryphal, we find reference to the north-bound migration of the Ten Tribes, which they undertook in accordance with a plan to escape the heathen by going to 'a farther country where never man dwelt, that they might there keep their statutes which they never kept in their own land.' The same writer informs us that they journeyed a year and a half into the north country, but he gives us evidence that many remained in the land of their captivity." (Ibid., pp. 324-25.)

With the blood of Israel thus scattered, people of all nations may hear and accept the gospel and receive of its blessings. In this remarkable manner, a vital phase of the promise to Abraham is fulfilled.

One of the clearest explanations of the scattering of Israel is given in the fifth chapter of Jacob in the Book of Mormon. Not only does Jacob illustrate both the scattering and gathering of Israel, but he also explains the transfusion and retransfusion of the life-giving fluid of both wild and tame olive trees, as they are grafted and regrafted upon each other. This clearly illustrates how Gentiles and Israelites have intermixed and how well Abraham's blood has been distributed abroad.

Again, it is a dramatic portrayal of the mercy of God, giving to all—even to the most disobedient—an opportunity to repent and be saved. Did he not say that he was sent to the sick, and that the well need no physician? And who is fully well, spiritually? Who is perfect but One?

Relate all of this now to the coming of both Elias and Moses to the Prophet Joseph Smith in the Kirtland Temple.

Elias brought the keys of Abraham's dispensation and specifically said that he was restoring the promises, "that in us and our seed all generations after us should be blessed." (D&C 110:12.) That speaks of present-day peoples of various nationalities coming into the Church now. And who are they? They are those of "every nation, and kindred, and tongue, and people" of whom the angel spoke. (Revelation 14:6.)

So the prophecies referred to the scattered sheep, but also to their being gathered. And how are they being gathered? Through the powers restored to Joseph Smith by Moses! He also came to the Prophet Joseph in the Kirtland Temple. He committed to the Prophet "the keys of the gathering of Israel from the four parts of the earth, and the leading of the ten tribes from the land of the north." (D&C 110:11.)

And how is this gathering proceeding? Through the preaching of the gospel! The descendants of Joseph are being gathered into the fold, on many fronts. Joseph's people are in two general groupings. One is the children of Ephraim, who are the vast majority of the Latter-day Saints. The other is the family of Manasseh, represented in the descendants of Lehi. There are now more than four million Latter-day Saints in the world.

The Jews are being gathered too. The Latter-day Saints have

nothing to do with their movement. The Jews themselves inaugurated it. And that is what caused their confrontation with the Arabs in Palestine.

There are about three million Jews in Palestine today. Conversion probably will not come to them before the second coming of Christ. (See D&C 45; Zechariah 13 and 14.)

The return of the tribes from the land of the north is described in the Doctrine and Covenants as follows:

"And they who are in the north countries shall come in remembrance before the Lord; and their prophets shall hear his voice, and shall no longer stay themselves; and they shall smite the rocks, and the ice shall flow down at their presence.

"And an highway shall be cast up in the midst of the great deep.

"Their enemies shall become a prey unto them.

"And in the barren deserts there shall come forth pools of living water; and the parched ground shall no longer be a thirsty land.

"And they shall bring forth their rich treasures unto the children of Ephraim, my servants.

"And the boundaries of the everlasting hills shall tremble at their presence.

"And there shall they fall down and be crowned with glory, even in Zion, by the hands of the servants of the Lord, even the children of Ephraim.

"And they shall be filled with songs of everlasting joy.

"Behold, this is the blessing of the everlasting God upon the tribes of Israel, and the richer blessing upon the head of Ephraim and his fellows.

"And they also of the tribe of Judah, after their pain shall be sanctified in holiness before the Lord, to dwell in his presence day and night, forever and ever." (D&C 133:26-35.)

It is noted that they will have prophets among them. The Prophet Joseph Smith indicated in his day that John the Revelator was then among the Ten Tribes, preparing them for their return.

So we see that the promises made to Abraham have direct and significant relationship to us who live today. This is the day of gathering. We have the keys of Elias of Abraham's day by which all the "seed" to the latest generation will be blessed through our preaching of the restored gospel. We have the keys of Moses to gather them. And we have the keys of Elijah to bless them with their temple work.

It all fits together in one great pattern.

So Abraham was not just a patriarch noted for having lived in ancient times and having walked and talked with God. He was not just a ''father of the faithful'' whose children would be numbered as the stars of heaven. He was not just a prophet in whose life there was a foreshadowing of the sacrifice of Christ.

He was one of the chosen of the hosts of heaven whose influence has been felt quietly but surely down through the centuries as nations have intermarried and mixed their blood—and his blood—so that everyone could receive his blessings, if they would believe and live the gospel.

His influence is obvious as we now gather Israel. It is felt as we preach to the gentiles who will be ''adopted'' into Abraham's line because of their faithfulness. We have seen the changes in their lives. It is abundantly clear, too, as varieties of nationalities enter the temples and there receive their blessings, each in his own tongue. It is a great modern miracle.

Abraham, therefore, is unique in all the annals of religious history. He is especially significant to us who now carry the restored gospel abroad. That gospel goes to all nations, tongues, and peoples in order to reach his descendants, those to whom his ancient promises mean so much in this modern day.

Over four million are now in the fold. Each year many thousands of others are added. Abraham's ''believing blood'' is important in their conversions. Through it faith and salvation are offered to all whether they are of the ''chosen race'' or not. It helps them recognize the voice of the Good Shepherd.

Abraham has given birth to nations, kings, and queens, but also to God's prophets who have carried the good word through the ages.

Many of them have sacrificed their lives in doing so, sealing their testimonies with their blood—and his! However, that was but a reminder of his own willingness to sacrifice Isaac. Abraham knew what sacrifice was, and now so do many of his faithful descendants.

Abraham was also represented in the Great Sacrifice. It was

he who became the favored progenitor of the Lord Jesus Christ. It was his line in which was born the Savior of the world, the Son of Almighty God.

So what of Abraham? God chose him as his friend!

Chapter 35

THE PRIESTHOOD LINE

The final extension of the blessings of Abraham—priesthood and temple—has been made. By revelation the Lord gave to President Spencer W. Kimball the good word that now all peoples, regardless of race or color, may receive the priesthood blessings. Following is the announcement made by the First Presidency June 9, 1978:

The First Presidency of The Church of Jesus Christ of Latter-day Saints today released the following statement:

As we have witnessed the expansion of the work of the Lord over the earth, we have been grateful that people of many nations have responded to the message of the restored gospel, and have joined the church in ever-increasing numbers. This, in turn, has inspired us with a desire to extend to every worthy member of the church all of the privileges and blessings which the gospel affords.

Aware of the promises made by the prophets and presidents of the church who have preceded us that at some time, in God's eternal plan, all of our brethren who are worthy may receive the priesthood, and witnessing the faithfulness of those from whom the priesthood has been withheld, we have pleaded long and earnestly in behalf of these, our faithful brethren, spending many hours in the upper room of the Temple supplicating the Lord for divine guidance.

He has heard our prayers, and by revelation has confirmed that the long-promised day has come when every faithful, worthy man in the church may receive the holy priesthood, with power to exercise its divine authority, and enjoy with his loved ones every blessing that flows therefrom, including the blessings of the temple. Accordingly, all worthy male members of the church may be ordained to the priesthood without regard for race or color. Priesthood leaders are instructed to follow the policy of carefully interviewing all candidates for ordination to either the Aaronic or Melchizedek Priesthood to insure that they meet the established standards for worthiness.

We declare with soberness that the Lord has now made known his will for the blessing of all his children throughout the earth who will hearken to the voice of his authorized servants, and prepare themselves to receive every blessing of the gospel.

Sincerely yours,

The First Presidency

Now in full fact is the gospel extended to every nation, kindred, tongue, and people. The restrictions of the past are lifted. The Lord again proves that all mankind are his children, with equal opportunity to become like him.

The full significance of the mission of Abraham may be beyond our finite comprehension, but it is obvious that his blessings are truly extended to those of every lineage.

How kind and gracious is the Lord. Now, no matter what we mortals may have done in our preexistence, he allows us this present opportunity to truly keep our second estate. If we do, we are promised that glory and progress shall be added upon us throughout the eternities.

EPILOGUE

And as surely as the Lord liveth, will he gather in from the four quarters of the earth all the remnant of the seed of Jacob, who are scattered abroad upon all the face of the earth.

And as he hath covenanted with all the house of Jacob, even so shall the covenant wherewith he hath covenanted with the house of Jacob be fulfilled in his own due time, unto the restoring all the house of Jacob unto the knowledge of the covenant that he hath covenanted with them.

And then shall they know their Redeemer, who is Jesus Christ, the Son of God; and then shall they be gathered in from the four quarters of the earth unto their own lands, from whence they have been dispersed; yea, as the Lord liveth so shall it be. Amen.

—3 Nephi 5:24-26

INDEX